Who Speaks for Hispanics?

Who Speaks for Hispanics?

Hispanic Interest Groups in Washington

Deirdre Martinez

SUNY
PRESS

Published by State University of New York Press, Albany

For information, contact State University of New York Press, Albany, NY
www.sunypress.edu

Production by Diane Ganeles
Marketing by Anne M. Valentine

Library of Congress Cataloging-in-Publication Data

Martinez, Deirdre.
    Who speaks for Hispanics? : Hispanic interest groups in Washington /
Deirdre Martinez.
        p. cm.
    Includes bibliographical references and index.
    ISBN 978-0-7914-9357-1 (hardcover : alk. paper) — ISBN 978-0-7914-9358-8
(papercover : alk. paper)   1. Hispanic Americans—Politics and government.
2. Hispanic Americans—Population.   3. Lobbying—United States—Case studies.
4. League of United Latin American Citizens.   5. National Council of La Raza.
I. Title.
    E184.S75M382   2009
    323.1168073—dc22

                                                                    2008018955

10 9 8 7 6 5 4 3 2 1

Contents

List of Figures   vii

Acknowledgments   ix

Chapter One: Introduction   1

Chapter Two: The Actors   19

Chapter Three: NCLR and LULAC   29

Chapter Four: Education Reform Efforts   89

Chapter Five: Goal Formation on Charter Schools   107

Chapter Six: Goal Formation on Immigration Reform   137

Chapter Seven: Conclusion   149

References   157

Index   169

Figures

1. Agenda-setting process   13

2. Proposed interest-group goal-formation process   16

3. Educational attainment rates   20

4. LULAC structure   39

5. Elected positions within LULAC   41

6. LULAC membership   57

7. NCLR organizational components   70

8. Organizational chart   72

9. NCLR leadership tenure and staffing   73

10. NCLR annual budget, 1974–2003   83

11. NCLR funding sources FY2004   83

12. Goal formation at NCLR on charter schools   122

13. Goal formation at LULAC on education policy   135

Acknowledgments

I am indebted to a number of individuals who made this book possible. I want to first thank the volunteers and staff at the National Council of La Raza and the League of United Latin American Citizens. They opened their office doors, filing cabinets, and minds to me and kept them open long after their patience really should have worn thin. Their dedication to improving the lives of Hispanics and the intelligent and thoughtful responses to my many questions were inspiring, and I am eternally grateful for their willingness to participate in this project. I would also like to thank the members of my doctoral committee. Margaret Goertz, my advisor and chair of my committee, provided very helpful and concrete guidance, and I thank her for pushing me to go just a little further. Matt Hartley offered direction at several critical stages of the dissertation, enabling me to move past the occasional difficult patch. Enrique Murillo was the unreserved supporter every dissertation committee should have; in addition to very useful feedback on an early version of the proposal, Dr. Murillo convinced me that I was doing something important and useful. Thank you finally to the very helpful staff at SUNY Press, whose assistance made this a better book.

1

Introduction

Latinos, now the largest minority group in the United States, have been described by the media on countless occasions as the "sleeping giant" of U.S. politics. Reviewing the existing research on Hispanics and their representation in the policy arena, one wonders if the somnambulists are not Hispanics themselves but those who study and write about policymaking. Hispanics share a history of discrimination and the problems of anti-immigrant sentiment and lack of progress in the American school system. How do they respond to these challenges? Who leads this diverse community? How do they make their voices heard in the policy-making process? On questions such as these, the literature is largely silent. This book takes two issues (namely, charter schools and immigration) and the two largest national Hispanic interest groups (the National Council of La Raza [NCLR] and the League of United Latin American Citizens [LULAC]) and reveals the character and substance of the leaders in the Hispanic advocacy community.

Interest groups are important players in Washington policy-making, and political leaders often look to membership organizations (a subset of the interest group world) for the support of particular American constituencies. Consider the influence wielded by an organization such as AARP, which in 2006 had thirty-eight million members and one billion dollars in revenue. Those considerable resources and its ability to mobilize huge numbers of older Americans on legislative issues make it a formidable voice for older Americans in Washington. Similarly, in the Hispanic community NCLR and LULAC, the two major membership organizations, are regularly courted by political hopefuls and are part of the policy-making process. At NCLR's 2005 conference, Senator Hillary Rodham Clinton remarked that "NCLR has for forty years been a strong voice insisting that the American dream knows no boundaries of language, color, or national

1

origin." At LULAC's 2005 national convention, the chairmen of the Democratic and Republican national committees were in attendance in an effort to court the members of the country's oldest Latino organization.

Among the major Hispanic interest groups, NCLR and LULAC are in many ways comparable; they have significant grassroots memberships, a strong presence in Washington, and are decades old. When they advocate for particular policy positions, the assumption is that they are speaking for the Hispanic community. Particularly as the number of voting Hispanics grows, politicians are only too happy to consider the views of these Hispanic leadership organizations, and may well assume that positions supported by organizations such as LULAC and NCLR reflect the will of Hispanics nationwide. Upon closer inspection, however, the organizations are strikingly different and take policy positions that would not have been predicted by looking just at their histories. For example, NCLR, generally thought of as an organization with strong ties to the Democratic Party, launched an aggressive campaign promoting charter schools, an issue whose support initially came from conservatives. Surprisingly, the historically more ideologically conservative and pro-Republican LULAC maintains a neutral if not hostile stance toward charter schools. In the debate over immigration, NCLR has over time moderated its position, while LULAC has moved from a conservative position to a much more radical one.

Who lead these organizations, and whom do they represent? Are they representing all Hispanics, or a particular subset who are their members? How do they form their policy positions, and what are the internal dynamics that affect their decision-making process? Political scientists know how interest groups form, attract, and retain members, and how their various strategies and tactics influence the policy process. Less well understood is the process sandwiched in between: how they choose from among various possible policy goals. What explains the adoption of controversial policy preferences? As these particular organizations work toward improving the lives of Hispanics, how do they decide which policies to endorse? Specifically, why would one Hispanic civil rights group support charter schools and another oppose them? Why have their positions on immigration varied? How these organizations make these agenda-setting decisions may help us understand whom exactly they represent. Are they representing a narrow band of community-based organizations, their members, or do they accurately reflect the interests of the larger Hispanic community?

As the Hispanic population grows and issues like immigration and language continue to capture the attention of citizens and legislators alike, a deeper understanding of these organizations is essential. Whether or not they accurately represent the views of the majority of Hispanics, while important, is almost beside the point; the reality is that they are perceived as leaders of the Hispanic community and will likely continue to represent Hispanics in Washington policy debates.

This book, using case studies of charter school and immigration policy, tries to provide a timely and informative portrait of the two largest and most widely known Hispanic interest groups. This aspect of the work should be of interest to a wide audience, including policy-makers, researchers and students in the public policy and Hispanic studies arenas, and the general public. The book also attempts to provide an important theoretical contribution, which will be of interest to those who study interest groups and public policy. By applying John Kingdon's multiple-streams model to interest-group decision-making, the book expands on Kingdon's valuable contribution and provides a new direction for the study of both interest groups and agenda-setting.

Definition of Terms

The term "interest group" is defined differently across various disciplines, and the term "Hispanic" is not well understood by all readers, so some definitions are in order.

Interest Group

The lack of disciplinary and cross-disciplinary consensus on the definition of an "interest group" contributes to difficulties evaluating and building on interest-group literature (Baumgartner and Leech 1998). In sociology, interest groups are defined by their voluntary nature and their intent to make demands on the government (Knoke 1989). Interest groups have been defined narrowly as collective-action organizations, "those who seek nonmarket solutions to particular individual or group problems, maintain formal criteria for membership on a voluntary basis, may employ persons under the authority of organizational leaders; and provide formally democratic procedures to involve members in policy decisions" (Knoke 1989, 7). Others recognize that interest groups may indeed pursue market solutions to group problems, and that their decision-making process may not be democratic. In addition, membership as a defining characteristic of an interest group is by no means universal; in political science, definitions vary widely. Interest groups have been defined broadly as those with organized representation in Washington, more narrowly as those organizations which have a voluntary membership base, and more practically as those groups which are part of a published directory, which can be the basis of an empirical study (Baumgartner and Jones 1993; Baumgartner and Leech 1998).

Often equated with interest groups, social-movement organizations have specifically been defined as formal complex organizations that identify with and seek to implement the goals of a broad social movement (McCarthy and Zald 1977). The political science approach to interest groups, however, is more interested in the organizations that have already successfully transitioned from challenger to established entity in the policy-making universe (Tilly 1978). Those interested specifically in political activity define interest groups as organizations that "seek joint ends through political action" and that "have collective goals that are politically relevant" (Schlozman and Tierney 1986, 10). This definition excludes organizations that do not attempt to affect policy outcomes, such as service-oriented nonprofits, and includes organizations in the private sector whose primary concern lies elsewhere but nevertheless have an interest in the policy process.

In order to address the variation in definitions used, numerous recently edited books have equated interest groups with "factions, organized interests, pressure groups, and special interests" (Cigler and Loomis 2002, 3) and with "special interests or factions" (Herrnson et al. 2005, xiiv). For the present volume, the definition of "interest group" is empirically derived; my interest is in studying the mature, major Hispanic membership organizations with headquarters in Washington DC. Therefore, the political science definition of an interest group as being a mature organization with organized representation in Washington whose mission involves seeking solutions for a particular group of people is appropriate.

Hispanic

The estimated Hispanic population of the United States as of July 1, 2006, was 43.7 million, 14.7% of the nation's total population, making people of Hispanic origin the nation's largest minority racial/ethnic group. But what does "Hispanic" really mean, and to whom is this a meaningful identity? Is "Latino" more appropriate? Or are the subgroups so different that any effort to lump them together is problematic (Baker et al. 2000)? Is it accurate or appropriate to collect such a diverse group into one catchall category?

In 1980, for the first time, individuals were asked to identify their race as well as whether or not they were of Hispanic origin on the decennial census. As defined by the U.S. Census Bureau, "Hispanic" refers to people whose place of origin is Mexico, Puerto Rico, Cuba, or Spanish-speaking Central or South American countries. The Census Bureau did not act alone; an advisory committee with significant representation from the Mexican American advocacy community was an active participant in the process of developing an inclusive term for individuals of Spanish origin (U.S. Census Bureau 2002). Hispanic political elites played a major role in the development and the acceptance of the "Hispanic" label (Gomez 1992). Elite Mexican American actors, including members of Congress and organizational leaders, readily admitted that they had begun to use the term "Hispanic" instead of "Chicano" by the early 1980s (Gomez 1992). Leaders found the use of "Hispanic" to more accurately represent the changing demographics of their constituencies. Others felt that the term "Chicano," in addition to referring only to Mexican Americans, was associated with a militant movement that was out of step with the more conservative political climate of the 1980s (Gomez 1992). Ethnic labels are also situationally mediated; a Puerto Rican may identify himself as a Puerto Rican in one context but as a Hispanic in another (Padilla 1986).

As to the character or identity of the Hispanic population, recent political debates and media portrayals might lead one to believe that the Hispanic population in the United States is dominated by very recent immigrants, most of whom crept over the border between the United States and Mexico in the dark of night. In fact, of the 43.7 million Hispanics, fully 60%—25.9 million—are native-born. The remaining 40% of Hispanics, about half of whom have arrived in the United States since 1990, come from many different countries, each with its own traditions and history. While Mexicans still make up the majority of Hispanics (65.5%), that lead is shrinking as other subgroups grow. There are increasingly significant numbers of Central and South Americans (14.2%), Puerto Ricans (8.6%), Cubans (3.7%), and other Hispanics (8.0%) (Owens 2006). Geographically, while more Hispanics continue to live in the West, they are also moving to cities and counties in the South and elsewhere that have never played host to Hispanics (Wortham et al. 2002; Hamann 2003). In 2006, a quarter of all Hispanics lived in the West (26.6%), but 14.5% Hispanics were living in the South and 11.5% in the Northeast. Looking at education, there are also differences between subgroups. While no Hispanic subgroup had high school graduation rates as high as non-Hispanic whites, there is considerable within-group variation; only half of Central Americans twenty-five years of age or over have completed high school, compared to eight in ten South Americans (50.5% of Central Americans, 82.6% of South Americans) (Owens 2006).

The profile above suggests wide disparities in the character or identity of the Hispanic population; but when socioeconomic issues are considered, they tend to share a great deal, especially when compared to the non-Hispanic population. They are twice as likely to lack health insurance, less than half as likely to have completed high school or obtained a bachelor's degree, and almost twice as likely to be living below the poverty line, when compared to non-Hispanics. In addition, Hispanics share cultural characteristics, such as familism and the importance of the Spanish language (Tatum 1997). Finally, there are also structural forces that lead to the creation of a politicized Hispanic/Latino identity (Padilla 1986; J. A. Garcia 2003). These include the shared burdens of discrimination, anti-immigrant sentiment, and educational underachievement.

The Gap in the Interest Group Literature

The very existence of interest groups has long posed a puzzle for political scientists. During the 1950s, pluralist theorists argued that individuals naturally mobilize to right felt wrongs or pursue collective goals (Truman 1951). In the 1960s, scholars rejected the assumption that all individuals had an equal ability to organize; as Schattschneider so eloquently states, "The flaw in the pluralist heaven is that the heavenly chorus sings with a strong upper class accent" (1960, 34). In a quite different microeconomic vein, Mancur Olson (1965) suggested that rational individuals are unlikely to join organizations if they could "free-ride" on the benefits of membership without paying their dues, and group formation was even less likely. But of course interest groups representing marginalized populations did form and survive. In the Hispanic community, several important organizations represent Hispanic interests in Washington, the courts, and in communities across the nation. Organizations such as these have shown they have the ability to attract members, maintain their organizations, and influence policy-making. On these subjects, a great deal has been written (Baumgartner and Leech 1998).

A close look at the study of interest groups over the last several decades reveals two major streams in the study of groups. The first—demand aggregation—has to do with how groups mobilize and how they attract and keep members. The second—group impact—covers what groups do and to what effect in the political arena. Following Olson, many of the questions asked and answered have occurred in the first arena. Within demand aggregation, scholars agree that much more is known about group mobilization than forty years ago (Baumgartner and Leech 1998). The various questions associated with the collective-action dilemma have been the focus of significant new findings. It is clear that groups do not have equal access to the political system, and that the interest group system is biased in important ways. The mobilization studies have made as much progress as they have because they share a unifying paradigm: the collective action logic laid out by Olson (Baumgartner and Leech 1998). They share a common theoretical outlook and a common set of questions.

Regarding group impact, studies—and, in particular, large-scale surveys—have documented the wide range of lobbying tactics and strategies that groups use to pursue their goals. While it is not entirely clear when groups choose particular tactics over others (grassroots activity versus face-to-face contacts in Washington, for instance), there is a solid understanding of the options available to organized interests in their pursuit of a goal. Less consensus exists on the influence of political action committees (PACs), with some studies finding considerable influence and others none at all (Cigler 1991), and the effect of lobbying activity has not been successfully measured (Baumgartner and Leech 1998).

While progress has been made in some areas, numerous authors have recognized a gap in the interest group literature—namely, how goals are formed. This process falls between the two main interests described above: how organizations form, attract, and maintain their membership, on the one hand, and how they affect public policy, on the other. The questions surrounding the internal organization of interest groups have been understudied (Berry 1994), and it is recognized that political scientists have not opened the organizational black box (Browne 1977). Tierney's comment on the subject exemplifies an increasingly recognized area in need of study: "How do organizations go about deciding what their interests are, and what policy goals should be pursued? In view of the centrality of this question to political science, it is striking that it has received relatively little attention" (1994, 38). The importance of goal formation has been acknowledged in the literature, but has rarely been addressed. In his important study *The Organization of Interests*, Moe says, "[T]he major value of a theory of interest groups derives from what it can say about group goals and, in particular, how they are formulated as a function of member goals" (1980, 73). Rothenberg finds that "the obvious logical inference to be derived from statements about how relevant goals are—that a voluminous, detailed literature exists that analyzes the importance of the internal operations of interest groups in goal formation— is incorrect. There is a dearth of empirical investigations, and only a modicum of theoretical work, inquiring into the crucial linkage between members and goals" (1992, 159; see Moe 1980).

Once an organization forms but before it develops a strategy to impact public policy, it must decide how to allocate resources as well as choose from among policy alternatives. These actions have been described as goal formation (Rothenberg 1992). The interest group literature does not identify "clear-cut decision rules" for the decision-making process within interest groups (Berry 1997, 90), and scholars have largely ignored the relationship between internal dynamics of groups and external lobbying activities (Gray and Lowery 1996). Anecdotal evidence suggests that many interest groups, when presented with a new policy debate, have an internal calculus that they use to decide what position to adopt. This involves asking questions such as:

- Will pursuing this goal or participating in this campaign benefit our constituency? Will it directly benefit our organization?
- What is the opportunity cost? Given limited resources, what are we sacrificing in order to pursue this policy goal?
- What is the net gain? How much of our resources do we have to expend and how does that relate to the potential gain?
- What are our chances for success?
- What is our added value? Is there another organization or coalition that is already pursuing this goal and if so, what do we contribute?

On this process and on the key variables that determine decision-making outcomes, the literature is virtually silent (Rothenberg 1992; Malen 2001). Citing the well-known ailments of the interest group literature—the methodological difficulties of the study of interest groups, the sporadic attention to the study of groups by scholars, and the fragmentation of the research—Lawrence Rothenberg proposes an integrated perspective on organizations (Rothenberg 1992). His study focuses on groups, not the interest group system, and pays close attention to issues regarding the role of the membership in goal formation, the conversion of contributors' preferences into goals, and the subsequent translation of goals into policy. Rothenberg suggests that these three domains of study within interest groups are related, though this is rarely recognized (more recent scholarship recognizes the interrelatedness of the influence-production process; see Lowery and Gray 2004). Several of his findings are relevant to the present book. First, membership is constrained by leadership decisions; any study of membership is incomplete without considering the motivations and actions of the organization's leadership. Second, goal formation can only be understood if the means by which the opinions of contributors—ranging from those of the individual to those of the foundation—are integrated into the analysis of these leadership decisions. Third, whether a group is influential or not and why an organization might choose to engage an issue on which it is not likely to be influential can be properly explained only if member motivations and the internal decision processes are understood.

Rothenberg tests both Olson's and Michels's theories by looking at the goal-formation process at Common Cause as it decides to pursue an anti-MX missile campaign. He reasons that based on Olson's logic, if there is no connection between members' preferences and a group's collective goods goals, goal formation will be accomplished largely by the organization's leadership, perhaps with input from some of the organization's more influential membership. Here we see that Olson's and Michels' theories are complementary; Olson predicts that the leadership would drive goal formation, and Michels suggests that the group's goals would move from radical toward moderate based on the leadership's desire to maintain a stable organization.

There have been considerable revisions to the Olsonian approach that suggest that organizational goals cannot be taken as the product of a dictatorship by group leaders, and Rothenberg confirms this view: "Once it is accepted that collective goods, purposive rewards, and member learning can play important roles in decision making, the likelihood that objectives are the result of an interactive process between members and leaders increases dramatically" (1992, 176). Rothenberg suggests, however, that there is a bias in the attention members receive; those who are more active or have more political or financial interest are more likely to be taken into consideration as groups form their goals. The study findings confirm his original hypotheses: "[L]eaders did not arbitrarily make decisions by themselves, shared interests were not taken for granted, and pure representative democracy was not practiced. Rather, activists' opinions were given special weight, credence was given to the views of other contributors, and leaders exercised discretion as well" (186). The findings reveal an interconnectedness between member preferences and the development of organizational goals. Building on Rothenberg's finding that understanding internal decision-making is critical to the study of interest groups, the present book revises John Kingdon's multiple-streams model and applies it at the organizational level.

Analytical Framework

The limited attention to goal formation within the study of interest groups requires exploration of other research areas that might provide guidance for this study. Organization theory is the obvious first area that must be explored. After careful review, organization theory provides only limited direction. March's *Primer on Decision Making* concludes: "The indeterminacies of decision intelligence and the complications in achieving it make the pursuit of decision intelligence frustrating. . . . modern theories of collective decision making over time are conspicuous for their failure to resolve such problems in the definition of decision intelligence" (March and Heath 1994, 270).

While organization theory itself did not provide a model, it did inspire the public policy theory, which I have in turn adapted to fit decision-making at the interest group level. Decision-making within organizations was first characterized using a stage-based, rational-choice model, which later evolved into a bounded rationality model. Working from bounded rationality, Michael Cohen, James March, and Johan Olsen (1972) developed a model in which ambiguity and inconsistency are the dominant characteristics of organizational decision-making: the garbage can theory. It is with the subsequent adaptation of the garbage can theory to explain agenda-setting in the public policy arena by John Kingdon (1984) that a potential model for understanding the goal-formation process in interest groups emerges.

The analytical framework for the present book takes the actors that interest group research suggests are important to goal formation and melds them with Kingdon's public-policy agenda-setting model. In this section I first summarize the actors identified in the interest group literature, provide a brief overview of organization theory, and then introduce Kingdon's agenda-setting model. Finally, I combine these elements in a framework that I use to guide my case study data collection and analysis.

Decision-Makers within Interest Groups

While goal formation has not been the focus of research on interest groups, multiple theories of interest group behavior can be applied to the goal-formation process.

- Member preferences: Building on Olson, Moe (1980) suggests that leaders will select policy alternatives preferred by members, or at least not offend those members.
- Patrons' interests: Influenced by Walker (1983), Marquez (2003b) and Ortiz (1991) claim that an organization's patrons (organizations or individuals who provide operating monies, such as foundations and corporations) will have significant influence, or at least the organization's leaders will not go against patrons' interests or preferences.
- Personal preferences of leaders: Michels (1958) argued that organizational leadership would make decisions that would ensure survival of the organization, with little regard for member preferences. While Sabatier and McLaughlin's (1990) commitment theory suggests that organization leaders are first and foremost committed to the goals of the organization, Ortiz (1991) makes a connection between Hispanic organization leaders' desire for organizational survival and career advancement and their approach to fund-raising.

These theories, however, assume the importance of one variable over all others. Rothenberg makes an important contribution when he identifies multiple variables in the goal-formation process. According to

Rothenberg, a subgroup of individuals, including the most active members, funding sources, and leaders, influence goal formation. The present book intends to build on Rothenberg's findings and improve our understanding of the goal-formation process.

Organization Theory, Garbage Cans, and Agenda-Setting

The idea that human beings rationally make decisions that are likely to optimally benefit themselves has heavily influenced the study of economics and much of social science, including the study of organizational decision-making (Green and Shapiro 1994). Rational-choice theory assumes that organizations make decisions based on four factors: a precise knowledge of the available alternatives, a full understanding of the consequences of each alternative, a set of consistent values that can be used to compare alternatives, and a decision rule that can be consistently used to choose from among alternatives (March 1999). In addition, numerous studies of organizational decision-making have assumed, as in the study of policy decision-making (Easton 1965), that the process occurs in stages (Mintzberg et al. 1976; Nutt 1984). Over decades, this rationality and orderliness have been moderated by some authors to reflect the reality of decision-making. Beginning with the classic article in the study of policy decision-making, Lindblom (1959) suggested that decision-making in organizations is neither rational nor comprehensive. Rather, he suggests that decision-making is done recursively in successive limited comparisons, given changing values, available alternatives, and limited information and resources.

A number of scholars pursued this argument, and have agreed that decision-makers in organizations are limited by the information available to them and the resources they are able to contribute to the decision-making process (Cyert and March 1992; March and Simon 1993). In addition to bounded rationality, organizational decision-making is further restricted by the presence of ambiguity. Preferences are not clear, are varied among the individual actors involved, and are likely to change over time (March 1999). This is best illustrated by garbage can theory (Cohen, March, and Olsen 1972; Cohen et al. 1986).

Garbage can theory attempts to explain the decision process in organizations characterized as "organized anarchies." These organizations are distinguished by three general properties. First, they have "problematic"—that is, inconsistent and ill-defined—preferences. Second, they operate under unclear technology—that is, their own processes are not understood by their members. Third, they suffer from fluid participation in decision-making as participants come and go due to time constraints and competing interests. This may not apply to the entire organization all of the time, but may describe a portion of an organization's activities.

A choice opportunity within an organization such as this can be described as a garbage can into which both problems and solutions are placed. There may be multiple cans available, and problems and solutions will be sorted depending on the availability of cans. A decision is the result of several independent streams of activity. Four streams are identified: problems, solutions, participants, and choice opportunities. This model suggests that problems and solutions are attached to choices not because this combination is the best alternative but because of their temporal proximity (March 1999).

Agenda-Setting: Streams, Windows, and Entrepreneurs

As in organizational decision-making, the policy-making process is complex. Multiple actors operating on a variety of levels play shifting roles over the decade or more involved in the institutionalization of a policy change (Sabatier 1999). Early analysis of the policy-making process focused on the work of government actors and assumed no external or environmental influences (Lasswell 1956). This framework was revised to include actors outside of government but who affect the agenda (Howlett and Ramesh 2003). Understanding the activities and interactions of policy actors both inside and outside of government is a key facet of understanding the policy process.

Numerous theoretical frameworks have been developed in the last several decades in an effort to explain and predict the policy process at the federal level. Developed by John Kingdon, multiple streams is one of seven major theoretical frameworks of the policy process (Sabatier 1999). Kingdon's model was influenced by the garbage can model (Cohen, March, and Olsen 1972). Going full circle, this study takes Kingdon's theoretical framework and applies it to the organizational level. While Kingdon and others who have subsequently used the model maintain that the policy process is complex and often ambiguous (Zahariadis 2003), the multiple streams framework provides more explanatory power than is possible if one conceptualizes the process as a garbage can, and it also enables us to systematically explore the organizational decision-making process.

The stages heuristic, a highly influential framework for studying the policy process, divides policy-making into a series of stages. Harold Lasswell first developed a framework of seven stages; more recently the stages have been divided into four broader categories—agenda-setting, policy formation and legitimation, implementation, and evaluation (Sabatier

1999). Unlike earlier work on the policy process, Kingdon goes beyond an examination of the stages to consider how one moves from one stage to the next; this method of transforming inputs into outputs has often been referred to as the "black box" of the policy process (Sabatier 1999). Taking the streams and the choice opportunity from garbage cans, Kingdon considers specifically the agenda-setting stage of the policy process. An agenda is a list of subjects to which officials are paying attention. The agenda-setting process narrows the set of subjects and allows subjects to move from the government agenda (those items to which people are paying attention) to the decision agenda (those primed for authoritative action). In effect, then, the agenda-setting process involves a series of decisions that result in the adoption or rejection of a policy alternative.

As illustrated in figure 1, five major elements shape the multiple-streams framework. The first three elements are the streams of problems, policy alternatives, and political activity. Policy windows, the fourth element, are opportunities for the coupling of streams; and policy entrepreneurs, the fifth element, are searching for opportunities—open windows or changes in streams—that will allow them to attach their solution to a problem. Each of these will be reviewed in turn, and the adaptation to the interest group level will be explained.

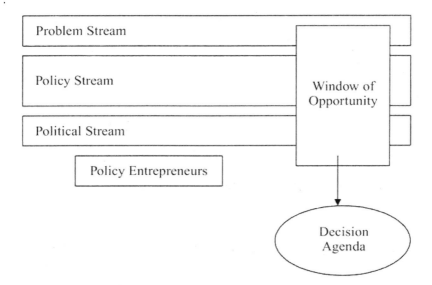

Figure 1. Agenda-setting process

THE PROBLEM STREAM

According to Kingdon, three factors can bring problems to the attention of government officials. First, the release of indicators such as poverty rates or educational attainment figures can cause an issue to surface in the problem stream. Second, a focusing event, such as a crisis or disaster, can also elevate an issue to a problem. The obvious example of this is the terrorist attack on 9/11 and the subsequent governmental attention to the problem of U.S. vulnerability to terrorism. Third, feedback, such as a review of a major federal program, can often provide a starting point that reveals a much larger problem ripe for action.

At the interest group level, group members are an important influence in the problem stream. Organizational leadership may observe a grassroots movement among their members and others to address a problem that had not been a priority for the organization. Leadership of a national organization may recognize a problem only after their local membership begins to clamor for assistance in their efforts to respond to a problem. Government action can also raise the status of a problem as a result of studies of existing programs or new policy proposals.

THE POLICY STREAM AND POLICY ENTREPRENEURS

The policy stream is where policy proposals are developed according to their own incentives and selection criteria. More vividly, Kingdon describes the development of policy proposals as a "primeval soup." Like biological natural selection, ideas develop and then fade, only to develop again, and may take considerable time to come to life. This activity occurs within a policy community, which includes all those actors in a given policy area. These specialists are policy entrepreneurs, recognized as an important part of the agenda-setting process (Kingdon 1984; Mintrom 1997). Similar to entrepreneurs in the economic marketplace, policy entrepreneurs attempt to bring their preferred solution to the government agenda. These are people willing to invest their resources in return for future policies they favor. They identify opportunities to attach their solution to a problem, and may adjust either their solution or the problem definition in order to reach the government agenda.

Within interest groups, policy proposals are developed or adapted by policy entrepreneurs who are interested in gaining organizational approval for their policy proposal or position on a policy debate within the organization. These entrepreneurs are also influenced by policy activity outside of the organization; they may latch on to a movement and revise the idea to meet their organization's (or membership's) needs. I also hypothesize that while entrepreneurs within an organization do not have the power to authorize pursuit of a policy alternative, once an alternative is endorsed by organization leadership the presence of a policy entrepreneur heavily influences the scope of the resulting project or initiative.

THE POLITICAL STREAM

The political stream is a powerful force for agenda-setting. A number of factors can influence the political stream, including a change in national mood or a change in presidential administration. Interest-group pressure campaigns can also spark activity in the political stream. As an idea gains momentum in the political stream, political actors build bargaining coalitions in order to ensure elements they consider vital are included in the policy change under consideration.

As in Kingdon's model, the political stream is critical at the interest group level. Policy entrepreneurs need the support of key decision-makers in order to develop their ideas into funded programs. Key actors in the political stream include the organization's board of directors and the staff with decision-making authority. While issues outside of the organization become defined as problems and move to the government agenda, organizations may feel compelled to respond to the alternatives being considered. Also, as the visibility of a policy alternative increases, new funding opportunities may arise. The preferences of funders may influence the extent to which an organization's leadership pursues a policy alternative. Leaders may also respond to pressure from members. Other factors that may influence the goal-formation process may include the ideological orientation of the group and the preferences of allies in the political process, especially elected officials or other groups.

WINDOW OF OPPORTUNITY

Kingdon finds that when the three streams are joined—that is, when there is complete coupling—problems are most likely to reach the decision agenda. This coupling occurs with the aid of a policy entrepreneur and, importantly, by the opening of a "window of opportunity." An open policy window could result from a regular reauthorization or some other major event in one of the streams. Open windows present opportunities for complete couplings. Kingdon suggests that windows open due to changes in the political stream or in the problem stream, when a problem captures the attention of officials. One revision to the streams model suggests that windows may not be temporary, as Kingdon proposes (Sharp 1994). In addition, Zahariadis (1996) suggests that when windows originate in the problem stream, they are likely to find a solution to a given problem, whereas windows originating in the political stream will search for a problem that fits an existing solution, because adopting policies is more important for a political actor than actually solving problems.

Windows of opportunity at the interest group level may result from a board or presidential initiative, a call from the membership for action on a problem, or an event outside of the organization, such as a change in presidential administration or an opportunity for funding. Funders, leaders, and members can all potentially play a role in the opening of the window or response to an open window. As in Kingdon's model, the window is most likely to open in the problem stream or the political stream.

Agenda-setting—the process by which problems are recognized, connected to a policy alternative or solution, and placed on the government agenda for action—has typically been applied to the government level. This case study finds that the framework Kingdon developed to illuminate the processes of agenda-setting and alternative specification can be applied to the goal-formation process at the interest group level. In order to accurately represent the process at the interest group level, the three groups identified by the interest group literature—funders, members, and leaders—must be included in the revised model. This is illustrated in the revised Kingdon model below (figure 2).

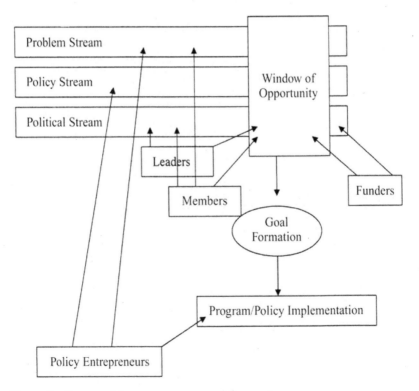

Figure 2. Proposed interest-group goal-formation process

This revised model makes it possible to test several theories of interest group behavior and determine if one of the three actors—members, funders, and leaders—alone drives goal formation as suggested by interest group theorists or if, as Rothenberg suggests, multiple interests interact. Combining these actors with the five variables in Kingdon's model adds complexity and provides a fuller picture of both the actors and the contexts that drive goal formation.

Methodology

Data collection began with a document review in order to establish the positions of the two organizations on charter schools and immigration and to determine what procedures if any were followed in the development of their position. I conducted preliminary interviews in spring 2004 at NCLR. These interviews were the beginning of an iterative process. Conversations with senior staff provided encouragement for my hypothesis that NCLR's endorsement of charter schools marked a change in its education agenda.

Formal interviews and additional document analyses reflect the framework I adapted for this study. The individuals interviewed fall into five categories: board members, organization leaders, organization members, organizational senior staff, and members of the education task force for each organization. Board member interviews provided insight into the activity in the political stream, the influence on decision-makers of activity in the problem stream, and the circumstances surrounding the window of opportunity. Organization leaders, as intermediaries between the boards and the staff, speak to the influence of funders, leaders, and members, and triangulate board members' comments regarding activity in the political and problem streams. Organizational senior staff provided further triangulation, and also shared knowledge of activity in the policy stream and the role of the policy entrepreneur. Members of the education task force were key informants on the window of opportunity, the policy stream, and the problem stream. Finally, organization members provided their perspective on the extent to which members' priorities are translated into organizational policy priorities. The influence of funders was determined through interviews with the range of interview participants. Twenty interviews were conducted for the NCLR case studies and fourteen interviews were conducted for the LULAC case studies. Using a semi-structured interview format and a detailed interview protocol, these interviews were sufficient to ensure compatibility across the cases. Substantial latitude was provided in the interview process for additional unforeseen information to be gathered. All informants were asked to provide written permission to record the interviews and use the material collected for publication.

The interviews lasted approximately one hour each. Some phone interviews were conducted when face-to-face meetings were not possible. Phone interviews and in-person interviews were recorded with permission. Interviews were transcribed for purposes of data analysis. To provide for anonymity, I have identified interviewees only by their organization and their general position within the organization (such as staff, board member, former board member).

Organization of the Book

Chapter 1 has presented the introduction, statement of the problem, a review of the relevant interest group literature, and methodology. Chapter 2 is an overview of the actors that influence policy-making on issues of concern to Hispanics, and provides further discussion of the decision to study NCLR and LULAC rather than any of the other national Hispanic organizations. Chapter 3 provides a detailed profile of the two interest groups that are the focus of this book: NCLR and LULAC. Chapter 4 lays out the history of Hispanic-education advocacy efforts in order to provide a context for the charter schools debate. Chapter 5 analyzes goal formation at National Council of La Raza and the League of United Latin American Citizens on charter schools, and chapter 6 offers a brief history of immigration policy and an analysis of goal formation on immigration policy at both organizations. Chapter 7 offers cross-site analyses and findings to emerge from the study as well as conclusions and recommendations for further study.

2

The Actors

In order to understand the activity and outcomes within the Hispanic policy arena, this chapter considers the variety of actors that participate in the policy-making process. Research explores the ability of Hispanics in elected positions to influence policy decisions of importance to Hispanics, and also the extent to which Hispanic elected officials represent Hispanic interests, as opposed to the interests of their general constituency. There is also evidence suggesting that community-based organizations play an important role locally and may have the potential to play a larger role at the state and national levels. Public opinion polls are increasingly targeting Hispanics, and are a valuable addition to the study of Hispanic policy interests. At the federal level, it is the national Hispanic interest groups that seem to have the potential to influence policy-making and that have been understudied.

Hispanic Public Opinion

According to a 2006 estimate, Latinos made up 36% of the 100 million increase in population in the United States in the last four decades (Pew Hispanic Center 2006). As their numbers have grown, the youthfulness of the Hispanic population suggests that education systems will have to be increasingly attentive to their needs; 34% of Hispanics were under eighteen in 2006, compared to 24% of white non-Hispanics (McKinnon 2003; Ramirez and de la Cruz 2003; Owens 2006). Over the next twenty-five years, the Hispanic population aged five to twenty-four is expected to increase by 82% (Pew Hispanic Center 2004a). As discussed earlier, although the majority of Hispanics were born in the United States, the problem of undocumented immigration has high visibility in the media and in policy debates. An estimated 11 million Hispanics are not documented immigrants; they either overstayed their visas or entered the country illegally.

Regardless of their immigration status, Hispanics are not succeeding in the American education system. Hispanics represented 16% of all those between sixteen and nineteen in 2000, but were nearly 34% of all high school dropouts of that age (Associated Press, October 11, 2002). As illustrated in figure 3, across the board, Hispanics are much less likely to succeed in education.

While each Hispanic subgroup has its own story with dramatically different histories, politics, and connections to the United States, low educational attainment cannot be explained by immigration or by national origin alone. Although looking at the group as a whole masks some subgroup differences, even the group with the highest educational attainment (South Americans) falls well below the rate for non-Hispanic whites (Therrien and Ramirez 2000). Also, while it is true that many Hispanic immigrants have not completed high school, even when excluding immigrant Hispanics from the dropout statistics, U.S.-born Hispanics are still much more likely to drop out than their non-Hispanic counterparts (U.S. Department of Education 2003).

A number of scholars have addressed the reasons for the disparity between Hispanics and non-Hispanics in educational achievement and have developed several theories to explain high minority dropout rates. The deficit model blames the individual, family, or culture for not instilling the necessary characteristics for success (Barrington and Hendricks 1989). The structural model looks to the school, and suggests that it is not designed to allow all students to succeed (Valenzuela 1999). Reproduction theory suggests that schools are instruments of the dominant group in society and so reproduce the inequality that exists in larger society because it is advantageous to the group in power to do so (Bourdieu and Passeron 1977). Finally, resistance theory suggests that individuals

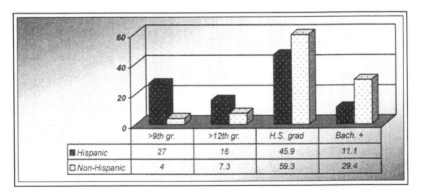

	>9th gr.	>12th gr.	H.S. grad	Bach. +
■ Hispanic	27	16	45.9	11.1
☐ Non-Hispanic	4	7.3	59.3	29.4

Figure 3. Educational attainment rates. *Source*: U.S. Census Bureau, Annual Demographic Supplement to the March 2002 Current Population Survey.

develop an identity that is not likely to lead to academic success because they do not think that graduating high school will improve their lives (Fordham and Ogbu 1986).

Regardless of the cause of low graduation rates for high school students and even lower college attendance, the implications are clear to many Hispanics, who consistently rank education as their top policy priority. Prior to the 1980s there was very little in the way of polling of the Hispanic population. With the adoption of the term "Hispanic" by the census, the growth of the Hispanic population, and their increasing influence in elections, the number of polls has increased, particularly in the last several years. Several of the recent polls ask respondents to rank the most important issues facing the Latino community. Going back to polls in the 1980s and up to the current day, education has consistently been identified among the top three most important issues facing Latinos, and often it ranks as the most important (Orfield 1986). A 2004 poll, conducted by Zogby International, surveyed 1,000 adults representing all Latino subgroups in all regions of the country. When asked to identify the most important issue facing the Latino community, more than one-third (34%) selected education, more than any other issue (Navarrete 2004). A poll from 2006 of Latinos in California found that 23% of those polled thought the quality of public education was the most important problem, followed by illegal immigration, at 14% (New America Media 2006). Another poll in 2006 found that 54% of registered Latinos said that education was extremely important in their decision-making regarding upcoming presidential elections, compared to 27% who said immigration was an extremely important issue in determining their vote for president (Pew Hispanic Center 2004b).

Looking specifically at education issues, concern over poor outcomes in education has been a constant, but opinion on particular alternatives has been limited. Polls in the 1980s found that although Hispanics were concerned about education, they did not have opinions or were not aware of models or programs that could improve outcomes, apart from bilingual education, on which opinion was mixed (Orfield 1986). A recent poll found support for vouchers and charters but also high percentages of respondents who did not know enough about the policy alternative to comment: vouchers were supported by 42% of Latinos, while 46% of those polled did not know enough about vouchers to comment (Pew Hispanic Center 2004b). Support for vouchers was halved (20%) when asked if they would support vouchers if it meant taking money from the public school system.

The second most frequent on the top-three list is immigration, trumping education in one recent poll. This 2006 poll found that 37% of Hispanics polled thought immigration was the most important problem facing Latinos, followed by discrimination (15%) and education (8%) (Latin Insights 2006). Another poll found that while only 8% of respondents suggested immigration was a top issue for Hispanics, 34% felt that discrimination was a major problem for Hispanics (Navarrete 2004). A poll in 2006 largely confirms that immigration tends to be recognized among the top problems for Hispanics; 14% of respondents cited immigration as "the most important problem facing the country today" (Suro and Escobar 2006). However, the same poll suggests that discrimination is a growing concern; 58% of respondents felt that discrimination was "a major problem that prevents Latinos in general from succeeding in America." A 2004 poll finds that most Hispanics are positive about the effects of undocumented immigrants on the U.S. economy (60%), and the vast majority of respondents (84%) supported the Democratic immigration proposal that would provide a clear path to citizenship for currently undocumented immigrants (Pew Hispanic Center 2004b).

The third issue is typically economic. A poll of Latinos in 2004 found that 23% of those polled felt that jobs and the economy were the most important issue facing them and their families, followed by education (17.8%) and immigration (13.3%) (Pew Hispanic Center 2004b).

Representation

Latinos work through multiple channels to improve educational outcomes and address discrimination. Groups, at different levels and using various mechanisms, are an important part of efforts to improve outcomes for Hispanics. Historically, national groups have intervened in the courts, lobbied the federal government, conducted policy analysis, and provided assistance to local groups. Local groups have served as advocates for Hispanic parents and their children and have also been important providers of direct service. The motivations and effectiveness of these various representatives are of particular interest. At the local level, do community-based organizations have the resources and capacity to effect change? Do Hispanic members of Congress represent Hispanics or are they focused on their general constituency, which may or may not be Hispanic? Do the national groups with memberships represent their particular members or do they pursue an agenda that benefits the larger Hispanic community? In the following section I review the sources of representation and advocacy in the Hispanic community, including local groups, school boards, Congress, and national organizations. While each of these groups provides potential avenues for research, I find that national organizations representing Hispanics are the appropriate focus for the present book. They have not been adequately assessed in the academic literature and, given their visibility, increasing access to resources, and history in the Hispanic community, are important actors in efforts to impact Hispanic outcomes. How they develop and pursue their goals is the subject of this study.

The Elected: School Board Representation

Research shows that the presence of Hispanics as school board members is a significant determinant of the number of Hispanic teachers in the district, which has a positive effect on Hispanic educational outcomes (Fraga et al. 1986). Hispanic representation in policy-making positions (school board members and education administrators) is associated with greater access to equal education; Hispanic students in districts with high rates of Hispanic leadership are more likely to participate in gifted courses, less likely to be assigned to remedial courses, and more likely to graduate from high school (Meier and Stewart 1991). Unfortunately, these same studies show that Hispanics are underrepresented on school boards (Fraga et al. 1986; Meier and Stewart 1991; Hess 2004). In a 2004 study, the boards sampled were 85.5% white, 7.8% African American, and 3.8% Hispanic. In the sample limited to large districts, which tend to be more urban and more racially heterogeneous, the figures are 78.9% White, 13.0% African-American, and 7.5% Hispanic (Hess 2004). The percentages in either case are significantly lower than the percentage of Hispanic youth in the population. Hispanics represent 12% of the entire U.S. population, and 16% of those between sixteen and nineteen years old.

Congress

In the 2006 elections, the number of Hispanics in Congress reached twenty-six, including two Hispanic senators, the first in thirty years. Political analysts suggest that Hispanic candidates have become more successful in recent years not because of the increasing clout of the Hispanic electorate but because of the increasing political experience of those Hispanics seeking office (Milligan 2004). Despite increases in the number of Hispanics elected to Congress, the evidence is mixed regarding the extent to which they represent Hispanic interests. A limited research base finds that while members of Congress did not directly represent Latino interests as measured by an analysis of roll call votes (de la Garza 1988; Hero and Tolbert 1995); there is some evidence of a collective "partisan" representation of Hispanics overall (Hero and Tolbert 1995). Researchers also note the limitations of considering only roll call votes, which ignore the influence of Latinos in bringing Latino issues to the agenda (Hero and Tolbert 1995). Future research in this vein might determine the extent to which the actions of particular Hispanic members and the Congressional Hispanic Caucus, as a group, address Hispanic concerns.

Hispanic Nonprofits

Compared to the rest of the nation's nonprofit sector, Latino nonprofits are largely regarded as a recent phenomenon. Only sixty-eight Latino nonprofits, representing less than 2% of those identified, were established during the first half of the twentieth century (Cortes 1999). By Cortes's estimates, currently there are approximately seven thousand Hispanic nonprofits nationwide. Reflecting an increased growth rate building since the late sixties, half of all Latino nonprofits are less than ten years old.

The majority of Hispanic nonprofits have less than $25,000 in annual income (62.4%), and only 6% have annual incomes of over $1 million (Cortes 1999). In testament to the larger and older Hispanic population in the Southwest, they are concentrated in California, Texas, and New Mexico, with smaller numbers in New York, Washington DC, and Florida.

LOCAL GROUPS

At the local level, there are thousands of Hispanic community-based organizations across the country that advocate, counsel, and provide direct service in Hispanic communities. NCLR lists 312 affiliates (all community-based organizations) in their network, with 70 in California. A senior staff member at NCLR characterizes the organizations this way: "If you were to tier up our networks right now, one tier would be very sophisticated, big-budget, multifaceted organizations. Next, there are mid-tier organizations with good budgets, and who have really taken a broader view of how they serve their community and have a solid financial base. The third tier is made up of small organizations, providing some basic information, and maybe offering one program."

As to their mission, Cortes finds their goals are diverse (1999). Many are concerned with veterans' affairs, providing scholarships, and promoting business. While many were organized to focus on education, others that originally intended to address immigration, housing, or other pressing concerns found that education was a major issue for Hispanics in their communities (D. Martinez 2002). A 1984 report summarizes the efforts of community-based organizations to stem the flow of Hispanics leaving high school without a diploma: "For individuals who have 'fallen through the cracks' in the public school system, the only safety net available in the Hispanic community has often been provided by Hispanic community-based organizations [CBOs]. . . . Hispanic CBOs provide an essential service in many communities, providing language training for those not fully proficient in English, teaching literacy skills, helping youth acquire high school equivalency diplomas . . . and encouraging youth to go on to college" (Orum 1984).

While their potential to change educational outcomes may be great, the available research suggests that their current capacity may be limited. Though there are older, more sophisticated organizations capable of significant fund-raising, most are new, small, and poorly funded (Cortes 1999). Cortes's findings overall suggest a lack of capacity among many Hispanic organizations to execute sophisticated reform efforts. However, as an interview respondent suggested earlier, there is also a "tier" of organizations capable of influencing policy-making at the local, state, and even national levels. Certainly there is evidence that individual community-based organizations have had remarkable success on a variety of fronts, including founding charter schools, energizing parents to reform schools, and offering youth programs that successfully guide disadvantaged students through high school. One example is the Parent Institute for Quality Education, a decades-old community-based organization in California that has developed a remarkably successful model that engages parents— including many new immigrant parents—in their child's school, which leads to dramatically higher rates of high school completion and college attendance. Another example of a community organization that has grown to serve the variety of needs of their community, Congreso de Latinos Unidos, Inc., in Philadelphia offers a range of services to the Hispanic community; Congreso's comprehensive services include HIV prevention, drug and alcohol counseling, afterschool and summer youth programs, welfare-to-work, and workforce development initiatives.

While the typical community-based organization began as a direct service organization and continues to focus on the day-to-day needs of its community, many are active participants in the public policy arena. In 1991, the principal at Denver's Valverde Elementary School disciplined students by making them sit on the floor to eat lunch. Parents learned that only Hispanic students received the punishment, and they bombarded the school with visits and phone calls. Their complaints ended the practice. In the process, Padres Unidos was formed. It was Padres Unidos that forced a three-year government probe into the Denver Public School System's bilingual education program. In November 1994, sixty-five parents filed a complaint with the U.S. Department of Education's Office for Civil Rights, accusing the system of wrongfully placing students with limited English proficiency in special-education classes, not employing enough qualified teachers, and not supplying students with adequate instructional materials. In 1997, the U.S. Department of Education's Office of Civil Rights ruled that the Denver Public Schools System's bilingual education program failed to adequately teach students with limited English speaking skills. By 1998, the program was under review by the U.S. Department of Justice. By 1999, Padres Unidos was weighing in on the selection of the next superintendent of Denver Public Schools and protecting illegal immigrant students from being arrested in school and then deported. More recently, the Hispanic Federation, a coalition of Hispanic organizations in New York City, organized a massive grassroots campaign to pressure newly elected House lawmakers to move quickly on immigration reform in 2007.

Additional research may find that there are a significant number of community-based organizations that are effective advocates at the state and local levels, and whose influence reaches to politics on the national level. I would tentatively suggest that community-based organizations are an important factor in the national response to charter schools in the Hispanic community; their influence in other arenas may be real, but have yet to be recorded.

NATIONAL GROUPS

Interest groups are important actors on the national stage. They fuel public debates on a multitude of issues like abortion, taxes, the environment, and education. Interest groups inform government leaders, publicize their opinions through the media, and encourage citizens to take action. The history and current activities of the Hispanic advocacy community suggest that they do have the potential to influence policy of concern to Hispanics. There are twenty-nine Hispanic advocacy organizations in Washington, ranging from established, well-known organizations serving all Hispanics to new and growing groups that focus on single issues, such as bilingual education, to single subgroups, such as Puerto Ricans, to single occupational groups, such as Hispanic nurses or fashion designers (CHCI 2000). While there are other organizations with headquarters in the West, their distance from Washington limits their involvement in policy campaigns on the national level.

The leading organizations in Washington, while using different strategies, have all historically pursued similar policy goals, particularly in the area of education reform. The oldest Hispanic organization, LULAC, led the pack by filing court cases charging discrimination in education (a detailed profile of LULAC is offered in the next chapter). In 1967, the Ford Foundation invested $2.2 million in creating a new organization, the Mexican American Legal Defense and Education Fund (MALDEF), which was modeled after the NAACP's legal defense fund. MALDEF filed the pathbreaking lawsuit in Corpus Christi that argued that the *Brown v. Board of Education* decision requiring desegregation of schools for African Americans should apply to Mexican Americans (Wilson 2003). Most recently, MALDEF represented one of three groups of plaintiffs in the successful school-finance case in Texas in which the judge found that the current school-finance system violates the Texas constitution because property-poor districts did not have substantially equal access to facilities funding and did not receive sufficient funding to educate their students (*West Orange Cove et al. v. Neeley*).

Finding that legislation and favorable court decisions resulting from the organization's litigation remain in many cases not fully implemented, in the 1990s MALDEF expanded its work to include community education, leadership development, advocacy, and parent empowerment. It is headquartered in Los Angeles, but has offices in Washington DC and eight other cities nationwide. Its net assets in 2003 were $13 million. It has a staff of three in Washington DC, a staff of thirty-six at their Los Angeles headquarters, and twenty-five staff members spread across the remaining eight offices.

Around the same time, Aspira (which means "aspire" in Spanish) was formed in 1967 in New York City by a group of Puerto Rican professionals and educators who felt that the surest route to reduction of poverty in the Puerto Rican community was education. Through seven independent state offices, Aspira offers a school-based leadership program providing leadership training, cultural enrichment activities, and community-action projects that teach students how to develop their abilities and become effective leaders in their communities. Two of its state offices operate charter schools. Its staff of seven in Washington coordinates national programs operated by the local offices and acts as liaison to the federal government.

A recent study that looked at the activity of minority advocacy groups at the congressional level identified LULAC, MALDEF, and NCLR as the three leading Hispanic organizations (Hero and Preuhs 2005). Specifically, over three decades beginning in 1970, these three organizations were called to testify at Congressional hearings over one hundred times each (Hero and Preuhs 2005). While it is not possible to definitively attribute policy change to their efforts, it is true that many of their policy priorities have been institutionalized; these include a federal bilingual education program, funding for migrant education, reform in school finance, and impact on immigration reform legislation. MALDEF was excluded from this book because I was interested in groups who were both membership organizations and playing a role in policy-making at the national level. MALDEF is not a membership organization, its headquarters is in Los Angeles, and its Washington office has a staff of three, which limits its ability to play a major role in policy-making. The next chapter looks closely at the NCLR and LULAC to identify their decision-making process and thereby to understand their policy positions on the two major issues for Hispanics today: education and immigration.

3

NCLR and LULAC

The research base on Hispanic organizations is limited, and the research available is largely critical. A summary of this research is offered, and is followed by original analysis of NCLR and LULAC.

Hispanic Organizations

The available research on Hispanic interest groups, particularly on NCLR and LULAC, largely responds to questions of demand aggregation—how the major Hispanic organizations have attracted and kept members, and how their responsiveness to members has changed over time. Several authors suggest that these organizations, with main sources of funding from foundations, corporations, and the government, do not accurately represent the views of individual members or the wider Hispanic population. This section summarizes the research in this area, beginning with Benjamin Marquez, who has written numerous books and articles on the subject, and moves to other authors who have made important contributions. The review reveals the limited nature of the research on Hispanic interest groups and suggests the need for additional study.

As stated earlier, the ideas of Olson, Weber, and Michels have influenced a great deal of subsequent research. As evidence mounted that these early theories were in many ways incomplete, scholars have nevertheless also continued to find value in pursuing their main questions: whether organizations suffer from an "iron law of oligarchy," whereby goals of organizational maintenance and career advancement by leaders displace broad social-change goals and democratic participation (Michels 1958), or whether organizations are motivated to provide selective benefits in the interest of maintaining membership at the expense of more radical reform goals (Olson 1965). Marquez's research on Hispanic organizations supports both theories; he argues that the leading national Hispanic organizations are no longer effective social change agents for many of the reasons suggested by early theorists (Marquez 1993, 2003a).

In a study of LULAC, Marquez states in the beginning of the book that the organization "evolved into one of the most important of all Mexican American civil rights organizations" (1993, 1). By the end of the book, however, LULAC "has long been marginal to the political process" (112). Incentive theory, Marquez explains, suggests that as organizations move from an early mobilizing stage to a more mature stage, the incentives required to maintain adequate levels of membership must change. Marquez argues that LULAC survives because it was able to change its incentive structure, such that the organization evolved from "an activist civil-rights group to a staff- or elite-dominated group that would devote much of its energies to continuity and survival" (7). Marquez concludes that broad-based civil rights organizations in the Mexican American community are in decline, and will soon be replaced by younger, more vibrant local organizations, the subject of his next book.

Marquez's later study of identity politics as practiced by four major Mexican American political organizations in the Southwest is a useful addition to the scant literature on the purpose and activities of regional Hispanic organizations. However, as part of his rationale for studying these groups, the author suggests that "multitask civil rights groups" are no longer an important part of Hispanic reform efforts and that "any organization attempting to rally a large membership base by using an all-inclusive political identity is unlikely to succeed for an extended period" (2003a, 6). He defines organizations at the national level such as MALDEF and NCLR as "elite driven organizations, heavily dependent upon philanthropic or corporate support and driven by their institutional concerns" and suggests that organizations such as LULAC have "long ceased to be important players in Mexican American politics" (22).

Marquez (2003b) also finds that funders, and particularly "Anglo-controlled" institutions, have a profound influence on the policy choices organizations such as NCLR make. His methodology, however, does not support such a strong claim. Marquez compares the amount of money the organizations in the study receive from foundation sources to income from membership dues. From this he concludes that the organizations rely on, and as a result are influenced by, a small number of funding sources and wealthy individuals, and are therefore disconnected from their membership. The most serious critique leveled against funded social-movement organizations is that they have a tenuous relationship to communities of interest and elevate a leadership cadre that is isolated from the people they claim to represent. In the cases of MALDEF and NCLR, Marquez suggests the services and advocacy that each provides are delivered without input of mass membership (341).

Ortiz also suggests an unhealthy relationship with funders. He argues that in reaction to the dramatic funding cutbacks in the Reagan era, Latino organizations adopted a "corporate grantsmanship and partnership strategy" (1991, 82), in which Latino leadership pursued partnerships with corporations interested in the Hispanic market. As a result, Latino organizations must perform the function of "amplification," publicly thanking their corporate sponsors for their generosity. Ortiz suggests that constraints on resources and the structure of organizations make this strategy a rational choice. NCLR, Ortiz says, became such an organization "largely as a result of abandoning the strategy of community organization" (92). He concludes that this strategic choice reflects a continuation of the strategy of accommodation on the part of Latino elites. While this strategy enables the survival of these organizations, it also supports capitalism and the image of corporations, suggesting that policy choices will be constrained by their strategic funding strategy.

Others have concluded that "goal transformation" is not an inevitable process for social movement organizations (Valdez 1988). The theory of goal transformation suggests that as organizations become more structured, they tend to accommodate themselves to the larger social system and lose their radical character. Valdez uses case studies of three Chicano organizations and finds that this transformation is not consistent across organizations but occurs in varying degrees, depending on the membership incentives on which the organization is based (Valdez 1988).

In addition to the above studies, several others such as Gutierrez 1986, Ospina et al. 2002, and Rodriguez 2002 touch upon goal formation or attempt an analysis of the major Hispanic groups. Unfortunately, they reveal a limited understanding of the organizations under study or are not sufficiently thorough to offer solid conclusions.

A study of Hispanic interest groups found that we continue to know very little about what these organizations do and how they do it (Campoamor et al. 1999). It is clear, however, that while there are some older, more sophisticated organizations capable of significant fund-raising (such as NCLR and LULAC), most are new, small, and poorly funded (Cortes 1999). De la Garza finds that Latinos have not developed a wide network of community-based groups that link average residents to each other or to mainstream society, and that Hispanic organizations are of low salience to Latinos; they report lower rates of involvement with Hispanic than with non-Hispanic groups, and few can name a Hispanic organization (de la Garza and Lu 1999).

Marquez and Ortiz argue that national Hispanic interest groups pursue only those political activities favored by corporations, foundations, and wealthy individuals. However, correlation is not causation. Simply because organizations receive more money from large funders than from members does not indicate bias toward funder preferences. This study suggests that without careful case studies of the groups in question, such strong statements cannot be made. If a researcher were to find, for example, that NCLR did not operate an antismoking campaign but took money from tobacco companies, it would not be accurate to suggest that the organization is co-opted by corporate interests. It is necessary to first understand the multiple variables that influence their goal-formation process before measuring the extent to which corporate interests drive interest group behavior.

League of United Latin American Citizens (LULAC)

Founded in 1929 by Mexican American community leaders in south Texas, LULAC has historically played a major role in school desegregation efforts, sponsors an annual civil rights conference, and conducts voter education and registration drives. At the local level, its service delivery is powered by LULAC councils, comprised of independent groups of members that vary in their goals and level of activity; some councils provide direct service such as tutoring or voter registration, while others offer scholarships that are matched by the national office. In 2004 its membership totaled 115,000 individuals, and its national office is operated by a staff of ten. It reported $2,000,000 in net assets in 2005.

LULAC is an organization strongly connected to the grassroots and reflects this characteristic in everything it does. This section explores the character of the organization, including how LULAC operates, who the important actors are, and how decisions are made. Particular areas of focus include the organization's history, structure, and ideology. Testing the hypotheses summarized in chapter 1, the roles of members, funders, and leaders are also explored. Fourteen individuals were interviewed for this section. This includes the three most senior members of the ten-member national staff, two past presidents, the current president, all of the regional vice presidents, and several state directors.

History

LULAC, one of the oldest Hispanic interest groups in the United States, has the oldest established presence at the national level. The organization, started in 1929 in south Texas, resulted from the consolidation of several smaller fraternal and self-help organizations serving Mexican Americans. LULAC has been characterized as a moderate-to-conservative organization whose original membership were professionals in the small Mexican

American middle class (Marquez 1989; Kaplowitz 2003). One senior staff member suggests its conservative approach in the beginning was a reaction to events occurring in Texas at the time: "If you go back to the beginning of LULAC, there was actually a minirevolution going on in Texas in which Mexicans in Texas were actually trying to secede from the union—this was put down violently by the Texas Rangers. In fact, LULAC talks about how more Hispanics were killed in the Southwest than African Americans were lynched in the South. So it was pretty violent and ugly and so the LULAC leaders saw this and thought the better strategy might be to emphasize our American-ness and ask for the rights given to other Americans."

Their strategy was two-pronged: first, by offering English language learning and citizenship classes and other assistance to Mexican Americans through their local offices, they sought to provide the tools necessary for Mexican Americans to be accepted as 'white' members of society. Second, they focused on fighting discrimination against Mexican Americans. A senior staff member I interviewed told me: "So that was the strategy used—show them we're patriotic and loyal to the country but at the same time really start pushing the civil rights cases that would allow Latinos to serve on juries and go to nonsegregated schools and have things like drinking fountains open to all. It was a long-running battle, and it was lots and lots of cases—school after school, drinking fountain after drinking fountain, one at a time." They argued not for a separate identity for Mexican Americans but for treatment equal to that received by other whites. This strategy would not change until well after the 1960s civil rights movement had taken hold.

As an all-volunteer organization with little funding, LULAC's work was limited to court cases of significance in the areas of education and civil rights and to demands for better representation of Mexican Americans in important positions within the federal bureaucracy. Its success in gaining such appointments in the Johnson and Nixon administrations has been cited as the one area of progress for Mexican Americans prior to the changes in the Voting Rights Act in 1975 (Kaplowitz 2003).

Several of the earliest court cases demanding equal treatment in schools were brought by LULAC, such as the *Independent School District v. Salvatierra* case, whose lead counsel representing Salvatierra were both founders of LULAC (Hernandez 1995). In 1931, parents of seventy-five mostly Mexican American children in the rural community of Lemon Grove, outside San Diego, supported by LULAC achieved the nation's first successful court challenge to school segregation (Cockcroft 1994). LULAC was also instrumental in the *Mendez v. Westminster School District* Case in 1946, which was an important precursor to *Brown v. Board of Education*, and brought the desegregation campaign to Texas in 1948 with the *Delgado v. Bastrop Independent School District* case (Hernandez 1995).

Consistent with their two-pronged approach (court cases and direct service), LULAC's earliest and longest-running program conducts fundraising to provide college scholarships to Latino youth. Originally, the program was operated individually by each council, with some councils developing very large programs. One current vice president, a self-described community activist, has been a volunteer for LULAC for twenty-five years. According to this board member, "In 1955 we made it a matching program where the national offices matches funds raised locally. Through the matching program we currently give out about a million dollars in scholarships a year, pretty much all over the United States. Some councils raise more funds than we are able to match, so we cut it off at $20,000 per council. Some councils actually raise hundreds of thousands of dollars."

LULAC also sponsored a committee on education that, among other things, encouraged parents to send their children to school. In 1957, LULAC sponsored its first "Little School of 400," a summer program that taught young children a vocabulary of four hundred English words that would help them succeed in school. Some argued that the approach accepted some amount of separation of Hispanics from white students (Hernandez 1995). Nevertheless, the program was a success; it received public and private support and served fifteen thousand students in the summer of 1960, and served as a model for the federal Head Start program.

In the 1960s, LULAC pursued funding from the Ford Foundation to establish a staffed legal program; according to a senior staff member, "[T]he Ford Foundation agreed and in fact, they doubled the amount we asked for but they asked that we diversify the board so that it wouldn't be controlled by LULAC, and that's how MALDEF started." While MALDEF has grown considerably over the years and is a separate organization, this senior staff member points out the continued relationship with MALDEF as representative of the LULAC model: "And it's good, I think, to have separately incorporated entities working on issues, because they can then dedicate themselves to that—it's too much for any organization to try to do everything. So that's how we expanded and still have an impact."

The organizations continue to work together when it makes sense to do so. A senior staff member remarks: "Our current president serves on the MALDEF board and others connected to LULAC also have connections to MALDEF, so there's a pretty long history there and still to this day, when MALDEF sues, they often use LULAC as a plaintiff. They're the attorneys and we're the litigants."

In the 1970s, LULAC was an intervener in several desegregation cases and also supported bilingual education. In 1973, grassroots activity led to the creation of the LULAC National Educational Service Centers (LNESC) in thirteen cities. The centers, now in seventeen sites and reaching twenty thousand students a year, sponsor the scholarship program, provide academic counseling to middle and high school students, and encourage greater participation in higher education through the federally funded Educational Talent Search, GEAR UP, and Upward Bound programs. LNESC's net assets in 2003 were just over $1 million. In effort to maintain control of the spin-offs LULAC develops, the bylaws were very clear regarding LNESC's connection to LULAC; LULAC board members are automatically LNESC board members. This strategy is a result of past experience with councils and spin-off organizations. A senior staff member explains:

> At LULAC sometimes, we start something and it gets away from us. For example, a council will start a project and it will at the outset be clearly a LULAC project; they'll have a LULAC shield out front—maybe like a learning center. Say that council has a change in leadership (due to an election) and it's not an amicable change. Since that learning center was started as a separate 501(c)(3), they'll say, "Well, we're going to keep this board but I don't like this guy so we'll drop the LULAC name" and so in some sense it's still controlled by LULAC, most of the board is still LULAC, but . . . So there was a lot of that that's happened and in the LNESC's case we made it so that the board cannot be changed without the approval of the national LULAC board. So we're sort of getting smart. It's funny, some of the older councils that broke away are still operated by LULAC folks, but they don't want LULAC national to have any control, and mainly because they don't want to have to abide by the election laws— they want to stay on the board.

Also in the 1970s LULAC developed and spun off a job training program, Project SER. In this instance, LULAC partnered with American GI Forum, which is based in Denver, Colorado. The SER network consists of forty-two separate 501(c)(3)s operating in more than two hundred offices in nineteen states, Puerto Rico, and the District of Columbia. The SER network serves more than one million individuals annually. LULAC members continue to participate in the operation of SER; LULAC board members are part of SER's board of directors. SER also offers a network of service providers that LULAC can use to deliver its programs. A senior staff member explains: "We use them to roll out programs—we opened twenty-three technology centers last year and we opened them in SER and LNESC offices. But we still have some control over the program, like the curriculum and the program objectives. Technically they're both separately incorporated and independent of LULAC, but they still operate as part of the family of organizations that we've created and so we still try to coordinate our activities."

Marquez argues that by the 1980s, "LULAC political and civil rights activities conducted by rank and file members were no longer a prominent part of the group's agenda" (Marquez 1993, 11). Rather, LULAC leadership was focused on fund-raising and survival. LULAC is accused as being "incapacitated by vaguely stated goals and an amorphous Latino identity" (112). Another author finds that internal dissension and leadership scandals have plagued the organization since the 1980s; the organization has struggled to maintain its focus and reputation (Hernandez 1995). Marquez documents the 1974 indictment by the LULAC supreme council and subsequent impeachment by the general assembly of the national president due to mismanagement of funds, and many years of financial hardship for the organization (Marquez 1993). In the late 1980s, the LULAC Foundation was charged with misappropriation of funds and was disbanded. But it was in 1991 that the organization may have reached its lowest point. At that time the national president faced federal charges for filing fraudulent alien amnesty applications through his immigrant services business. One past national president is very candid about LULAC's recent leadership: "The previous leadership just had a total lack of respect for the organization, and the accounting was a mess . . . and the foundation was not helping at all. They were using it for their own purposes, to travel and so on." Another former national president identifies the 1980s as a difficult time and also sees the early 1990s as a turning point for the organization: "As in any organization, we went through some times where our leadership wasn't the greatest. There was a scandal some time ago when one of our leaders was indicted. Before him, our leaders were just not operating in a business-like way . . . it was very casual. By 1994, the organization was broke."

Around this time, the leadership recognized the need to reassess their governing and leadership strategy, and subsequent leaders reenergized the organization. A past president told me:

> In 1994, Belen Robles started a solid financial strategy that was accountable, and we worked hard from 1994 to 1998 to build up the organization. . . . [T]he leadership that we've had in the last fifteen years has made sure that we have some continuity and flow of money coming into the organization to grow and be financially solid. And that we are free from any type of leadership that is not mindful of the health and well-being of the organization. So I think some of the criticisms of us were true in the 1980s when I think the leadership was using an outdated model of operating.

One past president recalls the situation when her term of office began and the efforts made during her tenure to turn the organization around:

When I came into office we had a budget deficit, some internal difficulties. So my main focus at that time was not only to develop a relationship with the public and the private sector but also to re-structure the organization to meet the needs of the day. So we computerized our membership and fiscal systems. Prior to that it was a paper organization; my predecessor sent me sixty-four boxes of material and even that wasn't really complete. So we worked hard to streamline the organization. We had a national treasurer and still do, but I hired a fiscal officer. And one of the most dramatic changes is that when I left office we had almost a quarter of a million dollars in the bank.

By the late-1990s, the organization's leadership was well on their way to resolving their financial challenges, and opened a permanent na-tional office in Washington DC. One vice president summarizes LULAC's recent history and suggests the value of having a grassroots membership when pursuing advocacy goals:

When I started with the organization, there were only chapters in six states, no budget and little money. There was scandal at some times, with people not turning in books or misspending money, twenty years ago. But . . . the three previous administrations . . . brought back the credibility of the organization on the national scene. [One president in the 1990s] also brought back corporate sponsorships, because she brought back accountability. She helped make the new LULAC. She opened the national office in Wash-ington, which for some reason we never had and really needed. So those types of things have enabled us to have a direct lobbying arm on Capitol Hill. Whereas NCLR is a wonderful research arm and a wonderful policy arm that helps the Hispanic community na-tionwide, their focus is definitely in Washington. In all of LULAC we only have twenty-five paid staff. And when you have thou-sands of members working at the grassroots, you have a great force, when you walk into a senator's office and you're represent-ing a bunch of people.

Looking across the organization's long history, the interviews suggest that LULAC experienced perhaps more than its share of internal difficul-ties, and stood at the precipice of dissolution on a number of occasions. There have also been a number of constants, such as the role of members and a commitment to education and civil rights issues. A past president says: "I think that the membership has been very effective in making our position known on critical issues. When LULAC was founded we determined that our battleground would be the courts and the ballot box. And that's still true. And that's a strength that we bring to Washington, because I think it's been recognized that the voting power of the Latino community is something to be reckoned with."

Organizational Structure

The present structure of LULAC has three main characteristics. First, as noted above, LULAC is a volunteer organization whose membership plays an active role in the operation of the organization. Second, LULAC is led by an elected leadership, which has far-reaching implications. Third, as a 501(c)(4) organization, its ability to fund-raise is constrained, which results in a small organization connected to program-driven 501(c)(3)s. Each of these will be explored in turn.

Before exploring these characteristics, a brief overview of the organization is in order. As illustrated in figure 4, LULAC is run by a national board of directors and an elected president. The national board of directors, made up of LULAC members who are all volunteers and who are elected annually at the national convention, is composed of: the current and immediate past president, the national treasurer, the national youth president; vice presidents for elderly, women, youth, and young adults; six regional vice presidents; and twenty-one state directors. Excluding the state directors, these positions are elected by a vote of the national assembly, which is composed of the national board members, all district directors, and certified delegates of the local councils. Each council is allowed a certain number of delegates depending on the size of the council's membership. The smallest councils are allowed three delegates, while the largest councils may send one delegate for every thirty members on their rolls. State directors are elected in any state with three or more councils. Each of these states elects a state board with a structure similar to the national board and with a similar voting process. At the local level, district directors are elected annually by council representatives in their district. District directors meet monthly with council representatives to receive reports of council activity and respond to any concerns or questions councils may have. The number of district directors in a state varies; Texas has twenty-two district directors, while some of the states with only a few councils may not have any.

As illustrated in figure 4, the national board influences decision-making in two offshoots: SER Jobs for Progress and LNESC. The board also appoints commissions and task forces, whose members are usually part of the national board but may include regular members and outside experts. The board, headed by the national president, directs the activities of the national office and receives input from local councils. As will be detailed

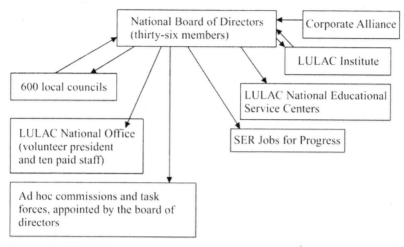

Figure 4. LULAC structure

later, the board additionally directs the activities of the LULAC Institute, which is the fund-raising arm of the organization. Finally, the corporate alliance was created in order to develop relationships with corporate America.

As suggested earlier, LULAC's national office, with its staff of ten, is deceptively small; projects spin off into separate but related organizations, and volunteers play a major role in the day-to-day work of the organization. As a senior staff member says: "That's really the LULAC strategy. From the beginning we focused on a volunteer army of people. We tried to get people involved in communities across the country to help, so our model is much closer to, say, the Boy Scouts with an advocacy bent than, say, NCLR, which is more of a paid staff or affiliate organization; they really aren't working with volunteers." For example, attorneys in Texas who are LULAC members have filed hundreds of cases on behalf of LULAC. A senior staff member remarked, "It's just incredible the amount of work. . . . They showed me a map of redistricting cases in Texas and the whole map is covered with dots. . . ."

LULAC councils hold voter registration drives, raise money to sponsor college scholarships, and provide numerous direct services such as tutoring and English language learning. Unlike NCLR, whose affiliates are formally recognized by the IRS as independent 501(c)(3) organizations and have paid staff, LULAC councils are made up of individuals who are volunteering their time. A vice president explains:

> Our councils are—you get a group of people—the minimum is
> ten—from all walks of life. They decide to join LULAC and form a

LULAC council. Those people decide their agenda—they are going to raise money for scholarships, or they all work at the same hospital and they are going to advocate for better conditions for Hispanic employees at the hospital. They may be members of a school district and they don't like the way that kids are being educated, so they form a council and they speak on behalf of the council. They are people who come from the grassroots, they are community people. Most councils have been formed because there is something that people don't like, and so they form to do something about it.

Several interview participants considered this a critical element for LULAC's longevity; one board member explains, "We're all volunteers . . . I think that's one of the reasons LULAC has lasted seventy-six years. There's a lot of autonomy—the local councils do what they want to do, as long as they abide by the LULAC constitution." This autonomy is reflected in the limited information LULAC collects on the makeup and activities of their councils. Councils, according to the current president, are a diverse group, including older, well-established organizations that have 501(c)(3) tax status and large budgets and very small councils with little or no funding that may hold one voter registration drive a year. While councils are required to pay dues and provide basic reporting data, they are largely free to manage their own affairs.

The volunteer nature of the organization extends from the smallest council to the national president. A past president explains the challenges of the volunteer nature of the presidency: "As a national president you travel four days a week and it's hard—you spend most Sundays at airports—it's a long four years—I accumulated a million points in frequent flyer miles. It's very difficult. You get to meet a lot of people, you get to do things that you wouldn't ordinarily do, but it's really a taxing volunteer job."

Interviewees also reported that the amount of energy volunteers can contribute to LULAC can change over time, which means that initiatives may not be fully implemented. A senior staff member finds that the volunteer nature of the organization can be a strength and a weakness. While this staff member suggested that the volunteers share a very important grassroots perspective, they also find that "[v]olunteers can't do it all. Unless you have staff in place to support them you can't do it all. For example, there was a paper that was supposed to come out last year and it never happened, because I didn't get the information I needed from members. . . . [T]hey are volunteers and their lives change. So people phase out for a while and come back in. . . . And that's the challenge with a volunteer group. So they might volunteer for a job and then they drop it after a year or even months because it's too much."

The second important factor in LULAC's structure results from the formal elections held to choose organization leadership across the orga-

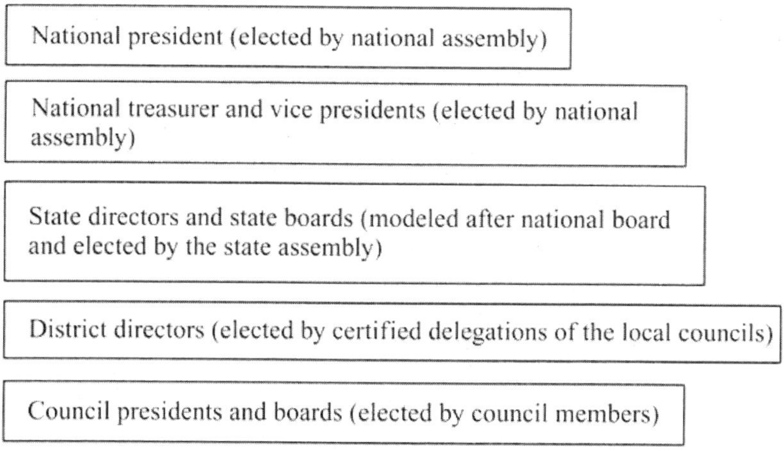

National president (elected by national assembly)

National treasurer and vice presidents (elected by national assembly)

State directors and state boards (modeled after national board and elected by the state assembly)

District directors (elected by certified delegations of the local councils)

Council presidents and boards (elected by council members)

Figure 5. Elected positions within LULAC

nization, and votes taken by the national assembly that establish the organization's policy positions. As illustrated in figure 5, all leadership positions in LULAC are elected. Each council holds annual elections for their own leadership, and members within the region elect their district and state leadership. As explained at the beginning of this section, each year at the annual conference the national assembly casts votes for the entire national board and the national president.

While interview participants universally supported the extent to which members were able to impact organizational decision-making, they also expressed concern that the electoral nature of the organization consumed a great deal of time and resources, pitted individuals and factions against one another, and made it difficult to develop long-term relationships with funders. On the positive side, a senior staff member points out the skills members obtain from the process: "In LULAC there's a lot of opportunity to run for office and have responsibility. You learn parliamentary procedure, you learn campaigning, and you learn leadership skills. And you get to be a spokesperson on that issue. So it really is a tremendous leadership development opportunity that we don't even talk about. LULAC itself is a program that has helped many leaders move forward. People like Raul Yzaguirre [former president of NCLR] and many members of Congress were LULAC members before they were anything else."

However, the political nature of the organization has multiple negative effects. It impacts the work of national staff, which must be careful not to favor one individual over another. As a past president explains,

They [staff] don't have the authority to act on behalf of the organization and the membership. And that's the way it should be;

the organization is very political and you've got to separate the politics from the work. I mean you have different people who want to be president—all the positions in LULAC are elected positions, and it's political from the national down to the council. So you have to be careful, because you have people who have been with the organization for a long time, and staff has to be careful not to take sides and remain independent.

Senior staff also suggest that their work is heavily influenced by the political nature of the organization, and this particular member of the staff has found it increasingly important to understand the local contexts of the LULAC councils in order to communicate effectively: "Everything in the organization is influenced by the politics. You not only have a lot of grassroots, you also have a lot of grasstops, with their own power base and local politics to consider."

Elections also impact LULAC's ability to maintain a focus and build relationships. One senior staff member candidly addresses the result of having an annual presidential election:

In some ways you could say that presidents get elected based on their positions on issues. Although it's not only that, it's also based on charisma, and on their ability to organize the councils. So a lot of the election outcomes are about turnout at the vote. The bad thing about the turnover in the presidency—sometimes as much as once a year—it can be destabilizing and I think that's why when some of the other groups were growing we weren't. You can't keep constantly changing the leadership and expect to grow. The other problem was that we didn't have a staff at all. The president would mostly start with new staff in the president's hometown every time.

This concern is echoed by others on the national board. One said: "La Raza gets a lot more—they have Murguia who will create a legacy and they had Yzaguirre. We have Flores, who is going to finish, so he disappears and then somebody else who might be an unknown is the next president. So there is no continuity there. A president has relationships with funders, and when the president leaves you have to start again. The national office and the president have to work a lot to keep that continuity."

Another board member concurred: "It's very bad to elect a president every year . . . to have the president run every year for office—he's got to basically stop what he's doing every year in January so that he can start running for reelection in July. And that's a weakness in the organization.

It's highly political. Sometimes that mix doesn't make for good policy." A third remarked: "A lot of energy gets consumed by the electoral nature of the organization. . . . I was of the opinion that the president's term should be a minimum of two years, because of the time it takes for a new leader to really grasp the entire area of responsibility. So that takes three to six months and then you have to start campaigning again!"

One former president discusses the political nature of the organization, and the fund-raising necessary to maintain a leadership position:

> This organization is all about politics. They [members] are all leaders in their own right. In their local communities, in their regions, and in their states. And they didn't get to those positions overnight. So you have to get all these individuals to work together instead of competing against each other—and that happens a lot around here—that's tough. There are turf battles and the fights over protocol—you better not mess up on the protocol. . . . I had to raise close to $40,000 each year to pay for events, goodies, buses from Texas, hotel rooms, to make sure they come to the convention . . . just to make sure if someone ran against me I would be able to knock them off.

One vice president points to activity that, while legal, impacts the ability of candidates to run for office: "I think that we really need to look at how individuals are elected. I mean you have individuals who raise their own money in order to campaign for an election. You have individuals running right now for the national presidency and they've raised $60,000 so that they can campaign. What if you have a really good candidate who doesn't have that kind of money? They go to the general assembly and the vote is already bought and paid for. And you end up expending a lot of energy on campaigning instead of on the issues."

At the local level, the organization's political nature can affect the functioning of the councils. As a vice president explains, "You're closer to some people than others, because there are a lot of people running for your position, so you create a lot of enemies too. This is an elected position, so there are people in your area who are running for your position, so there is a bit of conflict. There are people that I run against and then they won't speak to me because I won. So in your constituency you have people who are friendlier and then you have those who don't agree with you and they're less friendly."

One vice president indicates that members recognize the influence they hold within the organization, and are loath to change the system in any way that might jeopardize their decision-making power:

It's not the best structure, but our membership supports it. Our membership is very resistant to change. We have a constitution and it's an old constitution; over the years it has only been amended a few times. People don't even try to change it, because they know it won't go anywhere. There is a lot of conflict between different regional leaders who have different opinions. For example, the way we vote is open, so everyone knows who you vote for, and that creates tension. So we have been pushing for secret ballots, but people don't want to do that.

Another vice president confirms the recalcitrance of membership to change the basic framework under which the organization operates: "I've always said that it's easier to change the United States Constitution than to change the LULAC constitution. I think that's true. We're dealing with a constitution that's seventy-five years old. People don't want to mess with history. They have a deep respect for the founders, and they're very reluctant to change anything. But we have to change; even the U.S. Constitution has amendments."

This reluctance is reflected in the comments of a board member who at the time of this interview was embarking on a campaign to be LULAC's next president: "There have been some resolutions sometimes, like they want a paid president, or make other changes to the constitution. But as a whole it's worked out pretty well. The founders of the organization did such a great job, we can work with what we have."

One past president suggests that there not only appears to be real difficulty making changes to the constitution, but also that the election system may lead to elections that are essentially flawed. Marquez (1993) documents accusations of vote-buying, election fraud, and "paper councils"—namely, councils created solely to influence the outcome of elections. This past president I spoke to provides an example of potential voting irregularity and the difficulty in addressing such problems through amendments to the constitution:

I think the political aspect of the organization motivates the members to participate. On the other hand, I know that there have been several attempts to amend the constitution so that a regional vice president would be elected solely by those they represent—so only the members in the Southeast would vote for the vice president of that region, for example. And that would allow those members to select the leader they really want. The problem has been that as it is right now, there are these agreements that are made—you know if you vote for me I'll give you my vote. So consequently, the representative that you really don't want for your region gets elected because they manage to get the votes from people in other regions. Those amendments haven't passed. In fact, in the past few years, efforts to amend the constitution have not been processed as required so that they could be considered. So we have not had amendments to the constitution considered at the last two national conventions. I really have no explanation for that, though it seems that some individuals don't want any changes to the constitution.

One vice president confirms irregularities regarding amendments to the constitution: "Everybody says that we should make changes to the constitution, but when we try to make changes, the amendments seem to get lost. In the last couple of years, we submitted amendments following all the rules and nothing happened to them. The constitution really does need amending, and politics just gets in the way. We have to make people more accountable."

Another vice president suggests that electoral politics impacts the decisions board members make: "I get a lot of heat from other VPs who say, you're safe, you don't have any competition because you have to be a LULAC member for five years before serving on the board and in my region, and I'm the only one with five years so far. They clearly worry about getting unseated."

Elections, then, have a major impact on the work of the organization. Comments throughout the interview process revealed that paid staff felt they had to tread carefully so as not to offend an individual or group of individuals. Among the elected officials, it is clear that presidents expend considerable time and resources maintaining their elected positions. Among the general membership, it seems that members enjoy the power they hold through the elections process and are not willing to make any changes that would reduce their influence.

The third major factor in the structure of LULAC appears to be its tax status. According to the tax code, the IRC 501(c)(4) designation provides for exemption from taxation of the profit of civic leagues or organizations not organized for profit, but operated exclusively for the promotion of social welfare (Reilly et al. 2003). Contributions to LULAC are not tax deductible, since it is an organization designated by the IRS as a 501(c)(4). Charitable organizations described in section 501(c)(3), however, are eligible to receive tax-deductible contributions. The inability to receive tax-deductible donations has severely limited LULAC's fund-raising ability. According to a senior staff member, "With 501(c)(4) status, we can't apply for a lot of federal funding. Most of the time when you apply for funding you have to have 501(c)(3) status. Foundations, the federal departments, all want 501(c)(3) status." Like some of the board members, this senior staff member asserts that members are conservative in their decision-making when it comes to changes that would affect the core character of the organization: "I did check into what it would take to change to 501(c)(3) status, and the answer from the IRS was, basically, shut LULAC down and reopen it. Which I don't think the members would especially like—it's kind of dramatic. If we were to switch, then each council would have to be a 501(c)(3), and they would have to meet much more stringent IRS scrutiny; it gets a lot more complicated. So what we've done instead is create these separate entities."

In addition to LNESC and Project SER, LULAC has created a number of other 501(c)(3) organizations in order to improve its fund-raising ability while maintaining tighter control over the money that is raised. A senior staff member remarked:

> We created the LULAC Institute in 1996. And that's supposed to serve as the programmatic arm of the national office—all those programs that require a 501(c)(3) status—I guess we wanted something that we could hold a little closer to the national but still doing it exclusively for charitable purposes. Because what was happening was we've created all of these programs but then in the end the national office itself didn't have any programs— what ended up happening was all of the national office budget was overhead, we didn't have any program money in the budget. And we also wanted to start doing some things that required 501(c)(3) status; for instance, we're looking at purchasing office space here in Washington, but our potential sponsors would certainly rather contribute to a 501(c)(3) rather than making non-tax-deductible donations. And our convention even—a lot of that is educational in nature—and yet we couldn't receive charitable contributions for it. . . . [S]o it's been good for the national office to have the 501(c)(3) arm and not to have to go to another board and ask permission to do something. And also to have things not go as they wanted in some cases.

Despite attempts to keep strong connections between LULAC National and its spin-offs, Marquez found LULAC leadership in the 1980s frustrated with the lack of control that LULAC National had over its three major programs—LNESC, Project SER, and the LULAC Foundation. The latter never managed to raise significant funds for the national office, due in part, at least, to inordinately high operating expenses (Marquez 1993, 79). One senior staff member does not suggest the organizations are disconnected, but expresses frustration that fund-raising efforts by the national office tend to get spun off, leaving the national office to struggle with a limited funding base.

I think we could grow much bigger than we are, but we just don't have the staff and the time to go after the resources that are out there. The problem again is that we raise the money for something and then the board decides to create a separate 501(c)(3) so then the national offices loses control over that money. So none of this money that we're bringing in is adding staff to the national office so that we can handle more of the constituency requests that we get. My goal is to bring in new programs and hire new staff so that we can respond better to policy-related constituency requests. But it's tough.

From its beginnings, limited funds have determined the structure of the organization. The national office was staffed by volunteers; as the presidency rotated as often as every year, the national office would be relocated to the new president's hometown (Kaplowitz 2003). There was a national office for a few years in the early 1980s and a permanent national office was opened in 1997. The size of the Washington staff has not grown significantly since then. The current national office houses a staff of ten; there is an executive director and a director of policy and legislation. There is one individual who manages special events, including the annual conference that draws thousands of attendees, and one individual who manages relations with the ten thousand members. As one president suggests, there is an expectation that staff shoulder heavy workloads; "We don't have a very big national office. . . . We try to be as mean and lean as we can be and we try to squeeze as much blood as we can out of that turnip." One staff member suggests that members do not have a realistic understanding of the resources necessary to fulfill member expectations:

That's the hard part. If there's any danger, it's that there is an expectation of staff that far exceeds staffing capability at the moment. So the members will want to do, say, a major campaign on the minutemen [a vigilante group organized to stem undocumented immigration]. And they don't realize that to launch even one of the major campaigns they suggest I would have to hire staff. And because it is an elected board, they don't look at their role as raising money for the national office. If anything, they look at the national office as a resource for them to help their local councils. And perhaps even to win points for reelection purposes. So that's another challenge, because other boards will bring on a good fund-raiser or a good corporate person but we can't do that. If you want to be on LULAC's board, you've got to run. And most corporate reps wouldn't think about doing what you have to go through to be on the LULAC board; you've got to start at the beginning, build up a following, and do a lot of work. So the board does not help us with fund-raising.

Staff and members alike appear to be pulled in multiple directions. They tend to be fund-raisers, analysts, and program deliverers all in one. One vice president offers an example of a program delivered by Gabriela Lemus, who runs the policy component of the national office: "I know that Gabby raised money for a social security program; she was going to all the states and doing town halls. But they're small-time programs and they're limited and also it means Gabby is doing that and everything else she does. We all do a lot and it's great, but that's how we get burned out." Another vice president also suggests that staff is not sufficiently specialized: "At the national office, I would like for us to have a development coordinator. Someone who just deals with funding. On the policy side, I think we really need to be looking at health issues. But at the national office, you have one person doing all kinds of stuff and wearing all kinds of hats, and you just can't be effective that way."

These three elements—the volunteer nature of the organization, the elected leadership, and their 501(c)(4) tax status—in many ways define the modern LULAC. With limited ability to fund-raise and dependent on volunteers, advocacy and policy initiatives are constrained. Added to this is the jockeying for position that results from a membership that thrives on the political drama of annual elections. As later sections will reveal, decision-making is directly impacted by these factors.

Organizational Ideology

An organization's ideological position influences its advocacy strategy, aligns it with particular allies, and limits its access to actors and organizations not sharing the same political views. For example, initiated in the 1960s and influenced by the Chicano movement, MALDEF is perceived as a more radical organization that is less inclined to compromise its policy positions. Unlike MALDEF, LULAC was originally a conservative group, with strong ties to the Republican Party, and it pursued a strategy of accommodation rather than the aggressive approach adopted by the more militant Chicano groups. Throughout much of its early history, LULAC emphasized social, political, and economic justice and attempted to integrate Mexican Americans into American culture (Donato 1997). Clearly stated in its constitution is an allegiance to America, a trust in God, and an opposition to communism. Its first organizing guidelines limited membership to American citizens, excluding undocumented Mexican immigrants, and it declared English its official language (Hernandez 1995). In the late

1960s and into the 1970s, LULAC was heavily courted by the Republican Party, which saw the organization as an inroad to the increasingly important Hispanic voting bloc (Kaplowitz 2003). In the 1972 election, the Republican presidential candidate Richard Nixon won more than 50% of the Hispanic vote, and was endorsed by LULAC's national president.

LULAC, however, has often been ambivalent with regard to its assimilationist position; while it encouraged Mexican Americans to adopt white middle-class behaviors, it also asserted a clear cultural pride (Gross 2003) and pressed for federal programs that served the special needs of Mexican Americans well before the birth of the Chicano movement (Kaplowitz 2003). Reflecting the shifts in the organization's ideology over its history, a 2003 resolution called for the legalization of the four million undocumented Mexicans living in the United States, a position in stark contrast to the decision at the organization's beginning to limit membership to citizens of the United States. During the debate over immigration in 1986, LULAC adopted a tougher stance than NCLR, which decided that compromise would keep it at the bargaining table (Sierra 1991). LULAC has historically been a conservative, middle-class organization; but today's LULAC does not support charter schools, traditionally a conservative issue. Individuals within LULAC recognize that its ideological position does not look consistent to an outside observer. Some of this seemingly erratic behavior can be explained by the role of members in making policy decisions. Once members vote for a position, it becomes part of the organization's legislative platform and guides all future decision making on that issue. A senior staff member says: "[W]e try to stick to what members have asked us to do. And that gets people really mad at us a lot. The Democrats were really upset when we endorsed Leo Estrada, and the Bush folks were really mad when we opposed Judge Roberts. Those weren't member decisions, because they happened quickly. However, our position, which is part of our legislative platform, is that we support Hispanic appointments to the courts and administration; it's a long-standing position that's been voted on. So we take it seriously."

In the section that follows, the role of members in decision-making will be explored more comprehensively. But the individual acting as president exerts considerable ideological influence, as can be seen in the extent to which LULAC supported the George W. Bush administration. This is confirmed by a number of interview participants, who suggest that the president of the organization plays a crucial role in defining the ideological stance of the organization. A senior staff member has remarked, "I think the ideology shifts a little bit over time. I think the basic tenets of the organization stay the same—our priorities and our methods. But there are changes—we used to require U.S. citizenship to be a member, and we don't require that anymore. There is also an element of accommodation to the administration in power. Sometimes the pendulum will shift depending on who the president of the organization is and who the U.S. president is."

Looking at the last several decades, another senior staff member finds considerable presidential influence: "The presidents in the 1980s pushed the advocacy part of LULAC and pushed us in a much more progressive direction. If you look at the 1960s, we were sort of to the right of the Chicano movement—we were more of the middle-class group. But these guys definitely moved the organization farther to the left than we used to be. And I think that had a profound impact on us, because we're more progressive than we were in the 1970s."

A number of reasons have been provided for the influence of the organization's president. A senior staff member says, "The president has an enormous impact on the organization's ideology, for two reasons. One, they're given the microphone—the bully pulpit—and in some cases more than others they've gone forward on issues without necessarily checking in with the members, and so what happens is some members get angry and leave. And then maybe some that agree begin to come on board. So the public face of the organization is really helping to determine who stays in the organization and who goes."

One former president is less inclined to attribute ideological shifts to presidents, and suggests that LULAC does not fit an ideological category: "Politically, being Latinos, our members tend to be Democrats, but we have a good number of Republicans, too. But we try to stay neutral on politics. We can't afford to be seen as one—that's what has happened at MALDEF and La Raza, they're just too far to the left and they just can't function that way. Because any position they take people will say, Well, that's just because that's the Democratic position as opposed to really a position that's good for Latinos."

One vice president suggests that in addition to the influence of the presidents, a major shift within the membership is occurring:

> We're entering a period where the organizational dynamics of LULAC are changing. California and other areas are organizing like crazy. We think that a lot of the issues like the minutemen are actually the driving force behind people calling and wanting to join. Whereas in Texas and other areas you're seeing a pretty steep decline in membership. In the West, our members tend to be more moderate to liberal, and they tend to be Democrats. The balance of power is shifting from conservatives in the organization to moderates and liberals. And that's membership. Texas has lost significant numbers, and the West is picking up steam. It's a historic change, because now we're talking about several rising regions when it used to be one region that was big.

One former vice president suggests that the membership responds to the political dynamics of the times, leading to changes in the organization's ideological stance: "LULAC goes through progressive and conservative times. When I joined LULAC I thought it was too conservative for me. But as a friend told me when I started, this organization is what you make of it. Right now we're going through a progressive stage because really that's what we need right now, with immigration and education issues the way they are."

LULAC's ideology has clearly shifted over time. After the civil rights movement, membership became strongly tied to unions and the Democratic Party. Ideology appears to be somewhat fluid in the organization, as Republicans and Democrats appear equally able to win the organization's presidency.

Leaders

As discussed earlier, the organization is led by members who are volunteers and who have been elected to their positions on the national board. The professional staff, which is small, has limited ability to influence decision-making. Over the course of the interviews, it was not uncommon to find that the individuals in volunteer leadership positions had been LULAC members for twenty or thirty years. For example, Belen Robles became a LULAC member in 1957, and has held leadership positions at the local, state, and national levels. She was the national secretary from 1964 until 1970, when she ran for national president and lost because, she believes, the organization was not ready for a woman president. She was elected national vice president for the Southwest in 1974 as the first woman ever to be elected to that level of leadership. Serving in that position for four years, she then was elected as the national executive director, which was a volunteer position at the time. She was elected national president in 1994.

Interviews illustrate that this elite cadre—members who cycle through national board positions as their terms expire—is very influential within the organization. There are a few exceptions. Several board members, for instance, are relative newcomers, having been members for fifteen years or less. One vice president worries that the board is not renewing itself with an eye to the future: "We have a lot of longtime members, and actually I think we're having difficulty recruiting younger members. In the years that I've been involved in the LULAC board, I've noticed that it's mainly the same people. And it worries me that eventually LULAC may not be as powerful, because there aren't enough new people coming up."

Another relative newcomer on the board is also concerned that the national leadership is not sufficiently representative of the Hispanic population:

I'm concerned about where the organization is going to be in the near future. When I look at the board, I see some wonderful people who have been committed to LULAC for decades. But sometimes I wish some of these folks have had experience with other organizations, because I think sometimes we as an organization get stuck on our tradition and how things have always been and we don't appreciate how things are changing within the Hispanic community. The needs have shifted and changed and so, for example, while racism isn't the problem it used to be in Texas, it's really a problem in places like the Northwest.

The opposing view is that the national board requires members with experience and skills, and newer members may not have acquired the requisite skill set. A former president says of the political nature of the organization,

It's chaotic sometimes; you elect people and you don't have very good people to elect—say, in a region that doesn't have many councils—so you're stuck with people who are not used to being on a national board. Whereas in Texas and California, where we've been around a long time, you don't get elected to the board unless you've been part of LULAC for at least fifteen years. So you work your way up, and you get more experience before you get to the national board. In other regions you might have people on the board because they're the only ones that ran.

The elected nature of the organization's leadership provides opportunities to members who are not represented by the "typical" member profile; particularly in areas other than the Southwest, an increasing number of members are less likely to be Mexican American and more likely to be new to the United States. Some of these individuals use their elected position to advance their particular views within the organization. A board member remarks: "As board members, you are a participant at the national level and you can push your own agenda. Members of the board have different agendas; my agenda is illegal immigration and the new immigrants, and sometimes that has been overlooked because the people on the board have been second or third generation. I was born in El Salvador, so that's my agenda and I don't want them to forget that."

Interviews also revealed a disconnect between the members who comprised the organization's leadership and the paid leadership staff. Interviews suggested that while the work of the paid staff was respected, the staff were not recognized as part of the decision-making structure. One staff member complained, "The other challenge is I'm not always included in the meetings. So I find out after the fact what the priorities are.

That's starting to change, like the board is starting to ask me to be part of more of the meetings. But the communication between board and staff still needs to improve."

This staff member has adjusted to more directly meet the needs of members: "It's really interesting: when I go out in the field, which is frequently, I'm amazed at the disrespect they have for the Washington office. As if we are somehow not doing our job. Now with a staff as small as ours, it's really hard to meet the needs of every member. In response to that, I've changed my approach to the work, which is why I travel so much. I'm out of Washington fifteen to twenty days a month. It's really critical that I hear what the grassroots has to say so that I can communicate that on the Hill."

This staff member hopes this disconnect is something that can be addressed at the upcoming board strategic-planning session, to which staff have for the first time been invited. Further evidence of a lack of coordination between the board and the staff is the fact that the staff held a strategic planning session in November 2004, while the board conducted a separate planning session in December 2005. This staff member hoped the strategic planning session would have positive outcomes:

> I would like to see us create a set of short- and long-term goals that are very specific not only in terms of what we want to do in policy but also in how we work together. That ability between the staff and the board is really lacking. But I am hopeful, because there are new members and they are making it into leadership positions—after ten or fifteen years. That sounds like a long time, but you have to realize, some of our members have been with the organization from the 1940s. So there is a bit of a generational shift happening that I hope will lead to better connections between board and staff. I would like to see a commitment from the board that we engage in the work as a team. There's kind of an elitism, and we're just the hired help.

Several divisions among leadership became apparent over the course of the interviews. Board members from the Southwest, for example, were more likely to have been with the organization for decades and were perhaps more resistant to changing the organization in any way. Board members from the Northeast and Far West were not traditional LULAC members; they were less likely to be third-, fourth-, or fifth-generation Mexican American, as is the case in the Southwest. They were likely to be younger, newer to this country, possibly of Hispanic descent other than Mexican, and likely to have been with LULAC for less than a decade. These leaders were more vocal about needing to change the organization's operations so that younger members could play a greater role in the organization.

The organization also is divided between the volunteer leadership and the paid staff, particularly in Washington. It appears as though the more grassroots-oriented volunteer leadership that makes up the national board has a different approach to decision-making than the Washington-oriented paid staff. In interviews, staff tended to be very careful to remove themselves from organizational politics.

Members

While councils are diverse in their mission, activities, and makeup, there does appear to be a "typical" LULAC member, particularly in the Southwest. One senior staff member maintains that "people are second- and third-generation LULAC—whole families are involved. So they treat the LULAC convention like a family vacation. The other thing is people who may not be able to get into a leadership position elsewhere can still come into LULAC. It's kind of what you make of it. So folks that aren't necessarily polished still get to be a leader in LULAC. We provide a lot of access to folks that may not otherwise have that opportunity."

While some councils raise significant funds through corporate sponsorship, all members are required to contribute to their local LULAC council. The local councils, which currently total six hundred, receive dues from their members and pay dues to state and national offices. In return for dues, members receive selective benefits from the local LULAC councils, such as language and citizenship classes as well as social events and a newsletter. Interviews specify, however, that it is the intangible benefits that draw members. One member explains why he and others have committed themselves to the organization: "LULAC does a lot of good public policy, and so that's very attractive to a potential member when the other voices out there are private attorneys, or maybe MALDEF. But there isn't really a lot out there in terms of advocacy for civil rights cases and for public policy. There's NCLR, which is a sister organization of ours but it's not membership-based. Our organization is highly political, and you can work your way up to a level that gives you a lot of decision-making authority. That decision-making authority can lead to services for your community."

One former president also confirms that members tend to stay with the organization for decades, and also that many members, consistent with educational attainment rates among Hispanics overall, are not highly educated: "The LULAC member is usually a person who is working in the community or involved in the community. We have members who are educated, in the sense that they have some sort of career training, and then we have members who really are just grassroots people who are concerned with community."

In addition to new members from different Hispanic subgroups, one vice president suggests that a generational shift is also occurring: "The other changing dynamic is that most of the members who made the organization and gave it the numbers were WWII vets, and they're now passing on. And the new, progressive elements—teachers, doctors, lawyers—professionals— are joining LULAC now. And that's going to have a fundamental effect in years to come."

Because demographic data is not collected on membership, it is difficult to say with certainty whether the membership is adding significant numbers of younger members. Other board members suggest that the membership is still largely older, and sees a need to recruit new members. One said, "I'm looking forward to the strategic planning session so that we can talk about some of these issues, like the need for an expanded membership. We don't even keep data on our members and who they are demographically, but if you go to our national convention, at our general assembly, you can see that the majority of our membership are fifty-five and over. So that has implications for the future of the organization."

A former president agrees that the membership is older, and recognizes that a challenge to the organization is to make itself more attractive to younger members:

> I agree, the majority of people in leadership roles are over fifty and have been with the organization twenty or thirty years, but I see that changing. And these younger people have different ideas about how to work—you should see the e-mails they send, asking us what our position is on something and why we aren't involved on an issue. We're used to percolating everything from the local level and it takes a year to get to the national level— these younger people want us to respond quickly and to act. And we're not prepared to do that; we're just beginning to address it.

As discussed in the earlier section on organizational structure, some interview participants suggest that members wield great influence within LULAC; as a senior staff member states:

> When I say that members control what we do and what our positions are, we're serious about that. . . . And people don't understand that even though they've convinced LULAC's president on an issue, our position doesn't change. Companies get angry because they think we're friendly and maybe I've been nice to them, but then the membership decides to boycott them. There's these things and people say, Well, aren't you guys in control? And we say, Well, no, we're not! We're not in control. We run into these problems but I think in the end we really are representing the Latino community. So while maybe it's frustrating for policy types, it's what the community wants. They want an organization

they can control and speaks for them and is not afraid to take controversial positions and doesn't really weigh politics when coming up with a position on things.

The general membership's influence within the organization extends well beyond policy positions and leadership choices; members vote on the full range of decisions the organization must make. A senior staff member asserts: "And on some stuff, like where our convention is held, they may not be making decisions based on business analysis like other groups do. Little Rock, Arkansas, is a good example—it's not a place where the other groups would have thought to go, but we did. There are a few councils in Little Rock that kept trying year after year and they really sold it."

Unlike this staff member, one vice president suggests that the role of members is not as strategic as some in the organization might claim, and that changes at the national convention have weakened members' influence:

> The individual members used to be a lot more influential than they are now. They have to go through their representative now, but in the past the member used to actually set policy by going into the national convention and by voting on the organization's goals and objectives for the following year. Now you call your state officer or your local organization, they pass a resolution, and that resolution might make it all the way to the top. It wasn't a formal change, it was just a matter of the design of the convention program. I don't know if it was done on purpose . . .

Several interview participants confirm that in recent years, the structure of the convention has led to less member involvement in the development of the legislative platform. A former president explains:

> I won't say that the education agenda reflects totally the agenda for the national organization, because I don't know that there was sufficient input at this last national convention, that all the councils in all the different areas were represented. The business session was very short this year. When I was national president, we opened the business of the convention on Wednesday and we had general and committee meetings on all days. And this year as well as last year, only the committees met until the last day, when there was a general assembly. And although we did address all the resolutions that were submitted, other issues that were not covered by resolutions were kind of rushed.

This former president also highlights that regions with more councils may have more influence: "The way that the system of membership and representation works, depending on the numbers of councils in a region, their issues may be more likely to be heard. For instance, if you have three hundred councils in one area or state, and fewer elsewhere, the region with more members may have a little bit more clout."

Several interview participants point to Puerto Rico, however, as having a small number of councils that are very vocal about their concerns and seeing their concerns addressed. A past vice president has said: "Puerto Rico councils have a very interesting dynamic within LULAC. They bring a lot of issues to the table and they demand action—and I mean demand. They get a lot of bang for their buck. They're down to one hundred actual members now, with twenty-five delegates. But they get heard."

While a former president is clear that much of the strategic decision-making is left to the board, he is quick to explain the important role members play in deciding which issues the board should pursue: "The organization is founded on its members. This is an organization that really—the good work of LULAC happens at the council level in different cities and states throughout the country. They do most of the work there. There are some issues that develop—for instance, the minutemen in the border towns is an issue of national concern, so it comes up from the council level and it goes up the ladder to the national board and the national president, who initiate some type of policy initiative to deal with that situation or problem."

LULAC's membership has experienced peaks and valleys over its seventy-five-year history; in 1951 there were 3,300 members on the rolls, but by the late 1950s membership dropped to 2,800 (Marquez 1993). By 1972, LULAC had only 1,000 dues-paying members. In the 1980s, membership remained steady at approximately 4,500. By 2005, membership

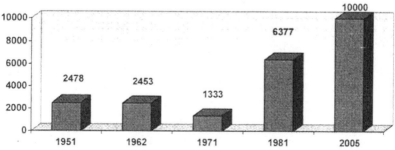

Figure 6. LULAC membership. *Sources*: For 1951–81 data: Marquez 1993; for membership number for 2005: Yarsinske 2005.

records indicate an increase to 10,000. Volunteers at the council level are required to donate their time and their resources and actively participate in the work of the council. A former president explains how the demands placed on volunteers constrain the organization's ability to attract new members: "We're not like other organizations where you pay your dues and you get a newsletter. Our organization requires that the councils meet, they have to do work, they have to pay dues. They volunteer, but they also pay to volunteer. They have to work. So it's difficult. It's not like La Raza that just has members that are other organizations. . . . Councils have to be functional, and unfortunately some of our members would get lax and not do things and the council would die. They have to be actively doing things."

A senior staff member suggests the election system impacts the number of members paying dues in a given year. On the positive side, elections keep the membership energized and active, as well as ensuring that LULAC is truly representative of its grassroots members:

> It keeps our community engaged and knowledgeable about the issues, and they are the ones who determine our positions on the issues—everything from the littlest things to the really big stuff comes from member votes. For us, when we speak, we're speaking on behalf of the community and not so much on behalf of a board or smaller group of people, because we're elected and representative. When you go to a LULAC national convention, there are on the order of eighty national resolutions that are passed on issues ranging from CAFTA to our position on the price of oil. And that's in addition to electing our leaders—every single leader, our entire board. And then there is the legislative platform, which is voted on, as well as amendments to the constitution. So the members have a tremendous amount of input. That's very different from other organizations.

On the negative side, members tend to participate when they feel their vote will be important to the outcome of an election, and may not participate when there is not a dramatic change looming or when they do not have an issue on which they feel the need to be vocal. This staff member continues:

> Membership numbers fluctuate based on what the elections are like that year. Which is another problem that we have. Sometimes a council will stay in existence, carry the LULAC name, and operate that council, but will decide not to send in their dues that year because they don't see anything exciting going on in terms of elections and so they figure they'll save the money and spend it

elsewhere. Right now, if there's a very competitive race for the national president this coming year, you might see higher membership rates. If it's a yawner—well, it depends . . . There are also some regions that are more susceptible to membership growth and shrinkage. Like, Puerto Rico at one point had two hundred councils and are now down to fifteen. They had a need for big numbers because they wanted to be heard, but right now they don't see the need.

A former president confirms that members may participate in the national assembly depending, more or less, on the elections to be held in a particular year: "The elections sometimes make the conference successful, because people like to go when there's something to be decided—it's the drama, it's the frenzy of everyone wanting to do something. This year, for example, with the [organizational] presidential election coming up, everybody is all excited, everyone is gearing up and trying to focus on a candidate and everyone is taking sides."

Members appear to have considerable influence within the organization. Through the resolutions process, members have established policy positions that organizational leadership must abide by. Despite changes in recent conventions, members also continue to wield influence through the election process. Candidates, responsive to the issues their supporters feel strongly about, recognize that the annual conventions are opportunities for their constituents to make sure candidates have honored their commitments.

Funders

At LULAC, members contribute a significant amount to the operation of the national office. In 2003, member dues paid to the national office totaled $129,000. The office also received funding in the form of non-tax-deductible donations from their annual legislative awards gala, in the amount of $265,000. The national office spends approximately what it receives from the gala and from membership dues each year on policy activity and constituent services. The LULAC Institute's net assets in 2003 were just under $1 million. This includes funding from approximately eighty sponsors, mostly corporate ones. LNESC's net assets in 2003 were just over $1 million, and Project SER programs varied, from $2.5 million in net assets in the SER office in Pennsylvania to deficits in other offices. In addition to national funding, LULAC councils and state offices conduct their own fund-raising. A current vice president statese: "It's also misleading to look at the national net assets, because all the states and councils raise their own money—Texas probably raises a million dollars a year on their own, whereas Washington State really doesn't have the resources yet. And there are individual councils who really raise significant dollars on their own."

As mentioned earlier, frequent changes in the national presidency may affect the organization's ability to develop relationships with funders. A former president recalls efforts to develop those relationships, and suggests that current funding does not reflect the organization's potential. This former president also pinpoints another area in which the elected nature of the organization affects how it functions: "I had an excellent relationship with funders. I was able to generate large sums. But I think we're still not there. We still have quite a ways to go. I don't see us getting big grants. I think we haven't yet recognized that we're worth it. I think you need to be able to be creative in how you approach the particular issue you're trying to resolve and develop a program that addresses it. And that's hard to do, because every LULAC region has different needs and priorities, and as an elected leadership you have to be sure you don't favor one region over the other."

Another former president suggests that while he made progress during his tenure, he also sees a need for continuity in funder relationships. After his tenure ends, he suggests his role will be to maintain his connections to funders: "I would like to continue working on the corporate side to bring more corporate partners to the table to help us. I always thought that we ought to tie in with corporations in longer-term arrangements. I see that I need to continue this—I don't want to lose the relationships that I've built in my time as a president."

A current vice president describes LULAC's fund-raising structure, and suggests fund-raising has been constrained by LULAC's policy decisions: "Every chapter in the organization is responsible for their own fund-raising, and they go out and do whatever they need to do to raise money for their program. And the state level is the same way. At the national level, we have boycotted Pizza Hut, we've boycotted other companies, and we've lost money over it. But there are other sponsors who know who we are and have stuck with us over the years."

A former president suggests that the organization's tax status has been a major constraint:

> The organization became a 501(c)(4) way back, and that precluded us from obtaining serious funding from the public or the private sector. It's true we created 501(c)(3)s to address certain issues like job training and education, but there were many issues that we couldn't address because of funding difficulties. So we created the LULAC Institute to be able to secure funds for those programs that the local councils could access. Most of the money derived from the LULAC convention and from grant writing

goes into the LULAC Institute, and then the councils are able to submit requests for funding.

Funding efforts may also be constrained because the organization does not devote sufficient resources to fund-raising. A current vice president says:

> I think sometimes it's hard to raise money for LULAC and even for LNESC, because funders want to give money to a program, not just give cash to a general fund. I think LULAC could raise more money at the federal level, but I don't think LULAC has the resources to do it. If LULAC were operated more like a company, there would be staff that would recruit members and raise money. The vice presidents are expected to do this, but they just don't have the time. We're volunteers, and you can only work so much. We give our vacation time to LULAC and we still don't have enough time to do everything that needs doing.

As seen elsewhere in this chapter, turnover in leadership, LULAC's tax status, and limited resources dedicated to program development and fund-raising have constrained fund-raising efforts at the national level. It was unclear from interviews if the availability of funding drove decision-making in other programmatic areas. The case of charter schools that follows may help reveal the extent to which the availability of funding impacts decision-making at the national level of the organization.

Goal Formation within LULAC

Over the course of the interviews, it became apparent that there are two ways in which goals are formed within LULAC: through the resolution process and by board member action. First, goals can be established through the resolution process as initiated by local members. In addition to voting for the leadership, members also submit policy positions in the form of resolutions to be voted on by the national assembly, which is made up of delegates from councils nationwide; and the assembly votes on the legislative platform each year. A former president explains the process:

> I would say that about 90% of all resolutions start at the local level. They are drafted by members of a council to address an issue of concern. Often they originate at the local level, but they are issues that have a national impact. Those issues are first addressed at the district level. If the resolution passes, it advances to the state level, and it is considered there. If it is of national scope, then it advances to the national level. There is a national committee that

reviews resolutions, and they allow proponents of the resolution
to come in and make their case. And then the committee votes
either to recommend adoption or rejection. And then it is presented to the national assembly.

Interviews suggest that, while it is true that members are able to pass
resolutions that in effect set organizational policy positions, resolutions
also undergo vetting that may not be based on thorough fact-finding.
One senior staff member describes the process used to decide resolutions
at the annual national conference. This description suggests that considerable decision-making is conducted in a very condensed time period:

> The resolutions committee gets hundreds of resolutions in, and
> we have two days to go through them all. The committee accepts
> or rejects resolutions. And that's based on history, prior resolu-
> tions, platform, and fit with our mission. For instance, I've re-
> jected resolutions that are asking us to support an organization
> I've never even heard of. If, at a later date, they've established a
> relationship with us, maybe then we will let that resolution go.
> But if it's some random thing, we don't let those go. We all have
> to agree on the committee. That can be very difficult. We've been
> trying to figure out how to streamline the process. . . . The voting
> process on the floor can take ten or twelve hours.

While the floor debate is very energetic and contributes to an engaged membership, the outcomes may lead to positions that are very different from what might be expected of an organization such as LULAC in
Washington. A senior staff member explains: "Your positions are decided
by the members, and they may not be the policy wonks, so maybe they
don't understand every issue, so you're getting more of a grassroots perspective on an issue versus a well-thought-out, analyze-the-details kind of
response. You as a result have a bit of a reputation for being somewhat
erratic. Sometimes we'll take a position that's considered rather liberal
and another time we'll take a very conservative view, and so Washington
folks don't really understand why we act the way we do."
    Other staff concur that LULAC's policy positions can be erratic; one
said, "I've tried to alter some of our positions to make sure they are consistent." While another staff member suggests that LULAC commands
the respect of policy-makers in Washington, as evidenced by the willingness of congressional leadership to meet with organizational leadership,
he also explains how the strength of the membership constrains LULAC's
ability to establish a presence in Washington: "There have been many
cases where I've felt bad about having to take a particular position. But

I'm not hired to make up policy; I'm hired to carry out the wishes of the membership. And even the board is supposed to abide by the decisions of the members—they cannot overrule the decisions of the national assembly; and so, if the national assembly has spoken on something they can't change it. The board's position on something is subject to approval by the national assembly—if the assembly decides to override the position of the board they can do it."

In addition to the general assembly process, the board appears to wield considerable decision-making authority. First, the board can act independently of the membership should an issue arise and require attention in between meetings of the general assembly. Second, board members feel that most of the resolutions passed by the membership provide a direction for the board to follow, but the board is responsible for determining the strategy to respond to the resolution. While most interview participants agreed that members are a strong voice in the organization, one former president suggests that while they provide the broad outlines, the president and the board have a great deal of decision-making authority:

I think the president's role is to dictate policy, to run the national office, to run the events we have, like the conference and the gala, and manage the agenda for the organization. Every year at the national convention the agenda is set out and it's up to the president to carry it out, to initiate projects and make sure that the agenda is being pushed. The president is the chair of the national board, and the president has a lot to say about which initiatives get brought to the board. . . . The agendas from the national assemblies are very broad; it's very rare that we get a specific order in the form of a resolution by the membership telling us to do something. They more typically just conceptually voice their concern about a problem and rely on the board to come up with a solution.

A current vice president also suggests that while members are heard, the board members are not simply channels for member decisions: "We are policy-makers on the board. We are an active board. Issues that come from my members through me, if they require national action, each vice president has the ability to bring that to the board. And then it's discussed in detail. Vice presidents reach out to others on the board for their advice and counsel. And then we come up with a plan of action on what we're going to do."

One recent national president provides an excellent example of the ability of organizational leadership to pursue their policy agenda even when there is not consensus within the organization on a particular issue.

During the debate leading up to the Central American Free Trade Agreement (CAFTA), the considerable pro-union element of the organization was opposed to the agreement, while other members were more supportive. The president was unable to reach consensus in favor of CAFTA on the national board, but he was able to deliver the support of LULAC in Texas, an important state in the CAFTA debate. Here he describes his position and the result of his lobbying efforts within LULAC: "I would rather we send the jobs to Central America than the jobs go to China. This was a very controversial issue within LULAC. In Texas we were able to sell it, but on the national board we were split down the middle. And without knowing we actually appeased both sides of the issue. With Texas in support—and Texas is an important place on this issue—we gave the administration the boost that they needed . . . three Hispanic congressmen out of Texas voted in support of it and it passed by two."

Another former president echoes the opinion that members play an important role in setting broad goals; however, the board and the president have a great deal of flexibility in implementation and in developing goals independently of members: "You get your policy direction to a certain degree from the membership at the general assembly during the national convention. But you are responsible for addressing issues that surface in the interim between conferences. You have an executive committee of board members and you also have the ability to implement policy through the national board. Whenever an issue surfaces that you believe will have national impact on the Latino community, then the president takes that up."

What comes out of the interviews, then, is the opinion that members are very influential through the voting process but also that board members are able to influence decision-making. One vice president indicates that the organization, in addition to being less responsive to member concerns than some of the organization's leadership suggests, does not have a clear decision making process. This leads to the erratic decision-making behavior one staff member described earlier:

> On policy decision-making, we're reacting to many things, instead of coming up with a well-thought-out policy response. When you have a small staff and issues come at you daily, many times you're forced to react. There are those of us in LULAC's executive board that want to build the national policy staff and in fact there are discussions taking place next month when we have a strategic planning meeting that I hope will address that weakness. . . . We want a process to decide positions, even positions that have to have quick resolution, that some thought goes into it. It's a wonderful organization, but in that respect it's broken. We are concerned with how we respond to policy issues—how effective we are on Capitol Hill. Are we one moment over

here with a liberal Supreme Court justice and the next, because it's politically good for us, we're approving someone with the opposite position? Those are the things we have to discuss.

Another vice president also suggests that decision-making by resolution has limited utility, and the outcome of the resolution process can be essentially ignored if the leadership is not inclined to act on a particular issue: "There isn't a real clear decision-making process. I mean the only time we really pass amendments or resolutions is at the national convention when we have the general assembly, and that's only once a year, and then you go home and you're so energized, and then nobody does anything; there's no follow-through."

A former president agrees that the decision-making process is not clear, and provides examples of resources that are commonly used to inform decision-making within organizational leadership: "The decision-making process may not be as well defined as it should be, and sometimes I know that things fall through the cracks. While our staff is limited, I know in my administration we had a tremendous network of people around the country who we could tap for advice. I surrounded myself with experts in a range of fields so that as an issue came up I could call on them for guidance."

A number of interview participants also recognized the need for research and policy analysis in order to inform their decision-making. One former active member remarks: "Without sufficient staff, we're really responding to issues as they come up. We have been talking about trying to be more research-based, but we haven't reached that yet." One former president recalls: "The national office staff has grown, though perhaps not as much as it should have. When I was national president, we did not have the policy staff we needed, so we entered into a memorandum of understanding with Raul Yzaguirre, because they have a tremendous research and policy arm, and we really needed that and we had the members. So we agreed when an issue came up they would share their research with us and we would assist in addressing the issue. That worked, at least while I was in office . . . ."

Comments from a former president revealed the weaknesses of the decision-making process. At one point in our interview his comments suggested that policy positions come from the local level and are vetted at multiple levels of the organization. He later admitted that some issues were not adequately researched. In a discussion of LULAC's position in support of No Child Left Behind, he suggests that more research should have been done: "The national office—we do not make our policy in isolation. . . . It starts down in the trenches, where locals create programs to deal with problems and then it percolates up from there to the district, the state, and then the national. Ultimately the chapter itself will do a resolution. Every year all these issues come to the table and the assembly itself discusses all these issues. And then the national staff also collects information on these issues. . . . On NCLB, it probably wasn't sufficiently researched or debated, because resolutions come up eighty at a time and there's just not enough time . . .

This former president recognizes the weakness of being driven by the grassroots on policy issues, but suggests, as others have, that the membership is not likely to change the decision-making method:

> So you have these two extremes—on the one hand, being in on the formulation of policy, versus now fighting them in the courts on constitutional grounds. Those are the two extremes, I would say. I think that you've got to look at these cases individually and not just be reactionary, and sometimes I think we don't spend enough time studying an issue—our people are always ready to boycott and demonstrate, and I think we need to be more willing to educate people on issues and be at the table. It's better than reacting—it's better to be on the front side . . . but you don't change the constitution. It's seventy-seven years old and you just don't change it. There's a lot of resistance. They don't want any changes at all. When you go to a meeting, members have a constitution in their pocket, and they will challenge you if you do anything outside of the constitution.

Officially, LULAC's goals are decided by its members. Through the general assembly, members vote annually on a legislative platform. However, this section has shown that board members feel they have the ability to shape LULAC's goals. In the case of CAFTA, leadership was able to accomplish policy aims without membership consensus. While members enjoy their ability to bring their local issues to the national table, leadership seem concerned that their decision-making process is not sufficiently informed and tends to be reactionary rather than thoughtful.

Conclusion

LULAC is an organization comprised of volunteers committed to improving the lives of Hispanics. Its dedication to its internal electoral process and a decision-making method that responds to the concerns of local members explains why its positions are not always predictable. The case studies of charter schools and immigration in the following chapters will be useful to identify the real impact of local members and the ability and willingness of national leadership to override member positions in the interest of having a place in national debates on policies that impact Hispanics generally.

NCLR

Like MALDEF, the Southwest (which became National) Council of La Raza (NCLR) began with critical resources from the Ford Foundation in 1968. Originally, the organization was meant to provide technical assistance to the many grassroots organizations that had begun to take root in Hispanic communities in the Southwest. In addition to this function, NCLR quickly became an important advocate in Washington DC on issues of concern to Hispanics. NCLR is now the largest national constituency-based Hispanic organization in the United States, with headquarters in Washington and eight field offices nationwide. NCLR continues to provide capacity-building assistance to over three hundred affiliated community-based organizations. It also conducts applied research, policy analysis, and advocacy, providing a Hispanic perspective on a range of issues including education, immigration, economic policy, housing, health, employment, and civil rights enforcement. Its staff is considerably larger than that of the other national Hispanic organizations, with a combined Washington and field staff of 125. Its net assets totaled $90 million in 2006.

While the history of reform efforts in the Hispanic community illuminates the roles of organizations such as MALDEF and LULAC in bringing court cases regarding desegregation, education finance, and other issues to light, the role of NCLR is not as clear. In fact, NCLR has not devoted considerable resources to the courts. Rather, it has developed its ability to influence Congress, the White House, agencies, and regulatory bodies. It is, of the Hispanic organizations, most notably the "inside the Beltway" player. Xavier Becerra, a member of Congress, active member of the Congressional Hispanic Caucus, and recognized leader in the Hispanic community, describes the organizations as follows: "LULAC is a grassroots organization with a tradition of cultivating local leadership and activism, and MALDEF is essentially a Latino version of the NAACP's legal operation. NCLR has a broader focus. It is a hybrid of a policy think tank with professional and effective lobbying capacity, a clearinghouse of best practices and development assistance for local and regional nonprofit community service organizations, and a fiscal agent for community-development institutions."

Becerra's definition of NCLR focuses on the defining characteristic of the organization. NCLR is, perhaps unintentionally, built on two pillars. One pillar is composed of its work in the policy arena; the other is its work in programs—that is, social service delivery at the local level. In many ways these two pillars also divide the actors; in the policy pillar, NCLR has developed a staff that is visible and well respected in Washington policy-making. In the program pillar, actors are likely to be deeply connected to the grassroots, which often advocates views more radical than the positions supported by the policy office. While the policy staff work to change the course of legislation or monitor the implementation of law, the grassroots may wonder how that work is connected to what the local groups do on a daily basis. This profile will explore in detail how NCLR functions, with one foot in the Beltway and the other firmly planted outside.

History and Structure

NCLR today is an organization with "$90 million in assets, an annual budget of $28 million, a staff of 125, and perhaps most important, is one of the nation's most prominent Hispanic-American advocacy organizations" (Crampton 2004). Its thirty-year history reveals a few peaks and valleys but an overall growth and formation of a solid reputation on the national scene. This section summarizes this growth and development and offers a detailed description of the organization's structure.

In the early days of the movement to improve opportunities for Hispanics in the United States, Hispanics had neither the network nor the resources that the black community did. African Americans had a longer history of organized struggle; they used their churches to mobilize, and they were able to obtain resources from the government in order to build their organizations and pursue their goals (Gallegos and O'Neill 1991). This imbalance was redressed in large part by the Ford Foundation—largely due to the work of Paul Ylvisaker, Ford's director of public affairs programs, and S. M. Miller, who succeeded him. It committed considerable resources to creating new national level organizations in the Hispanic community: "The Ford Foundation's support of the National Council of La Raza, Aspira, eight locally based community development organizations, the Mexican American Legal Defense and Education Fund, the Southwest Voter Registration Project, and a variety of research and specially targeted projects undoubtedly enabled Hispanics to develop permanent institutions that survive today and form a firm base for expanding social, economic, and political influence on a national scale" (Nicolau and Santiestevan 1991). As the organization developed, it was able to grow out of its dependency on Ford Foundation funding by obtaining contracts from the government to provide technical assistance to local groups. With this change, it was able to fund-raise in the corporate and foundation sectors.

NCLR's mission, unchanged since 1968, is "to reduce poverty and discrimination and improve life opportunities for Hispanic Americans" (National Council of La Raza 1999). Its work is divided into four major services: capacity building of community-based organizations, research and policy analysis, public information efforts, and special projects, such as its free trade project in the early 1990s. Topic areas that have received continuous staffing and resources include immigration, education, housing, civil rights, and poverty.

The history of the organization can be broken down into several periods of growth. Raul Yzaguirre, who retired in 2005 after being president of NCLR for the previous thirty years, sees four stages of development. From 1968, the year the organization was started, to 1973, the organization was searching for its identity and mission. This early period was marked by uncertainty and reliance on Ford Foundation funding. Several researchers found that Ford Foundation funding priorities drove NCLR's move to engage in economic development projects, an area in which it had little experience (Sierra 1983; Ospina et al. 2002). In 1973 the council moved its headquarters from Phoenix to Washington DC (Ford Foundation 1975), and in 1974 Yzaguirre was chosen to head the organization, marking the beginning of the second stage. Funding came in large part from the Carter administration (Sierra 1983). In that period, according to Yzaguirre, "We defined who we were and what we wanted to do and tried to put resources behind it to give that vision meaning. Those resources were largely federal resources." The decade of the 1980s marked the third period of development. By 1981, with the election of Ronald Reagan, federal resources all but disappeared. "We had to figure out a way to do our work relying almost solely on private funds. Foundations and corporations. To be more entrepreneurial in what we did," says Yzaguirre. The fourth and current stage began in 1992 and was marked, according to Yzaguirre, by consolidation in its national office and an expansion of its focus on affiliates: "In 1992 we began to worry about internal infrastructure and capacity and a changed relationship with affiliates where we became more of grantor than just a simple technical-assistance provider."

The modern NCLR is headquartered in Washington DC, where it has a large professional staff housed in a recently purchased building within sight of the White House. As illustrated in figure 7, NCLR is governed by an appointed board of directors and a president and CEO, and its staff is directed by one senior vice president and four vice presidents. The board also receives guidance from an affiliate advisory council and a corporate board of advisors. In addition to its Washington office, NCLR has field offices in Atlanta, Chicago, Los Angeles, Phoenix, Sacramento, San Antonio, New York City, and San Juan, Puerto Rico. Their sizes and scopes vary considerably. The Atlanta office, which opened in 2002, serves the Southeast region, which has thirty-nine affiliates. The office has one staff person and one program, the Georgia Latino Health Agenda. In California, home to seventy affiliates, there are several offices, including a policy office, a program office, and a center for health issues. Field offices hold annual regional affiliate meetings, in order to collect information on the work of the affiliates and to determine what role NCLR might play.

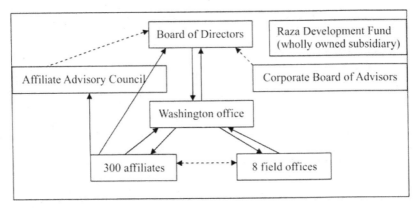

Figure 7. NCLR organizational components

NCLR's network of three hundred nationwide affiliates connects it to the local level. The network is divided into six regions: the Northeast, the Southeast, the Midwest, the Far West, Texas, and California. NCLR's affiliates are self-governed, independent, Hispanic-serving community-based organizations that offer a wide variety of services to their neighborhoods, including: education and workforce development programs; public health centers; Head Start centers and other activities for children and youth; financial services information; housing counseling; church-based ministries; social, relief, and refugee services; and legal/immigration services. Affiliates join NCLR because it provides them with access to technical resources and expertise, policy guidance and advocacy assistance, and funding opportunities. Affiliates are represented by the Affiliate Advisory Council and by their presence on the board of directors.

The Affiliate Advisory Council is comprised of two members (one male and one female) from each NCLR region. Members are democratically elected by the affiliates in their respective regions. Council members meet with affiliates in their regions twice a year to provide an update on NCLR's activities and to hear from affiliates. A board member representing affiliates also acts as liaison to the Affiliate Advisory Council. That person communicates to the board the concerns and needs of affiliates, and keeps the Affiliate Council Advisors up-to-date on the activities of NCLR.

Affiliates are increasingly benefiting from access to capital through the Raza Development Fund—the nation's largest Hispanic community-development financial institution and a wholly owned subsidiary of NCLR. In 2004 alone, the Raza Development Fund approved $16.5 million in loans to affiliates for charter schools, health centers, community facilities, and affordable housing units. The Raza Development Fund is governed by a separate board, though board membership includes some of NCLR's leadership.

NCLR's board and organizational leadership work closely together; the board provides counsel to staff, and with input from staff votes on any decisions that would significantly change the work of the organization. The board of directors currently has twenty-six members; this number ranges from twenty to forty, depending on the needs of the organization. The executive staff and the executive committee of the board identify the current needs of the organization and seek to fill board positions with individuals who can assist in those areas. Board members are appointed by a vote of the full board. One staff member says: "Right now some of our top priorities concern marketing and finance, so we're looking for people who can bring that expertise to the table." Board members are expected to meet twice a year; while some board members do just that, others invest considerably more time in the functioning of the organization. In the last decade, the board has appointed several task forces when NCLR leadership has found they are dealing with new or particularly challenging issues. Task forces are led by board members, who may appoint outside experts to the task force, and are staffed by professional staff within NCLR. The task force conducts roundtables or hearings, generates commission papers, and produces findings that are submitted for consideration to the full board. In 1992, a task force on international policy was developed to respond to NAFTA. The board also established a task force on women in 1993, and the task force on education was formed in late 1996.

In addition to input from task forces, the NCLR board gets guidance from the Corporate Board of Advisors (CBA). Established in 1982, the CBA is made up of senior executives from twenty-five major corporations. CBA members assist NCLR and its network through financial, in-kind, and programmatic support. One senior staff member suggests that the focus of the Corporate Board of Advisors has evolved:

> When the CBA was first initiated, it was an opportunity for Raul Yzaguirre to gather corporate leaders together to have intimate conversations about the relationship between corporate America and the Hispanic community. And that went very well. Raul is very well respected by corporate America and so I think there was a real willingness on the part of corporate interests to listen and participate. . . . It then evolved, in that the focus of working with the CBA had been on our special events—corporate sponsorships of things like our conference. More recently, there's been a shift. The CBA themselves want to be more engaged in our work outside of just providing financial support.

The Corporate Board of Advisors, however, has no voting authority, and is not represented on the board of directors.

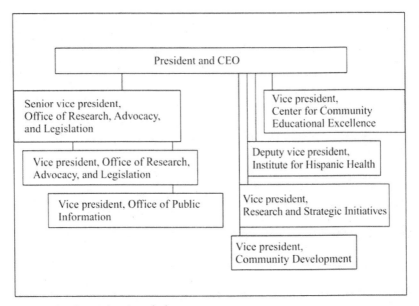

Figure 8. Organizational chart

The above description suggests a broad organization with sources of influence spread throughout the staff, volunteers, and affiliates. Structurally, the organization is divided into two main components: programs and policy. A senior staff member says: "I see NCLR as two pillars or two columns that hold NCLR. One is the advocacy pillar and that's the role we play in policy, advocacy, and research; that is a strong pillar. The other is our programs and services, because we support and oversee programs in education, workforce development, health, and community development."

The most clearly defined department within the organization is the Office of Research, Advocacy, and Legislation, which is the policy arm. Led by senior vice president Charles Kamasaki, this office has experienced gradual growth in its staff and is the most visible aspect of the organization's presence in Washington. As the organizational chart below shows, all staff charged with research, advocacy, the media, and publications report to Kamasaki.

Many of the senior policy staff are well known by congressional staff and other advocacy groups in Washington. A senior staff member remarks:

> NCLR policy analysts are recognized as among the more effective public interest representatives in Washington DC. Policy analysts conduct research, analyze legislation and regulations, publish formal policy analyses, prepare and deliver congressional testimony,

represent NCLR and the Hispanic community generally on Capitol Hill, and brief policy-makers and the press. Notable among the fifty or so NCLR Policy Analysis Center "alumni" are a state senator in California, the former director of congressional and legislative affairs at the Equal Employment Opportunity Commission, a senior lobbyist for the Diabetes Association, at least two college professors, numerous congressional staff, and many who hold other prestigious positions in the public, public interest, and private sectors.

Due to its size, resources, and Washington expertise, NCLR often takes a leading role in coalitions of Hispanic and non-Hispanic advocacy groups. Unlike other advocacy organizations, which might have at best one staff person to cover an issue area, such as education (and more often one staff person is responsible for multiple issue areas), NCLR has multiple staff members working on its major issue areas. This enables it to remain focused on the range of issues when other organizations can only focus on the most pressing needs.

In addition to the depth of the staffing in its policy office, an important factor in the growth and development of the organization, particularly on the policy side, is the longevity of key staff. As figure 9 shows, Raul Yzaguirre was president of the organization for thirty years, and many of his senior staff have been with NCLR for fifteen or more years. Particularly on the policy side, this continuity in staffing and the size of

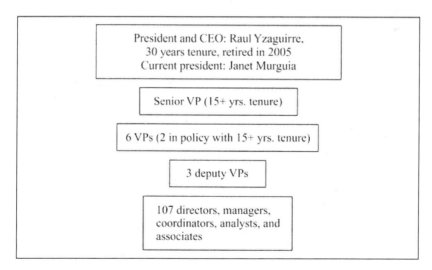

Figure 9. NCLR leadership tenure and staffing

their staff has allowed NCLR to establish relationships with funders, with other Washington advocates, and with political representatives. As a result of stronger funding relationships and greater resources, the staff have been able to dedicate considerably more time and energy to legislative advocacy than other Hispanic groups, and subsequently often lead advocacy campaigns in the Hispanic advocacy community.

Unfortunately, Yzaguirre's long tenure did not have a similar effect on the programs division, whose size has not been as stable over the years. Perhaps due to the vagaries of funding explored in the next section, programs have come and gone, leaving a flatter reporting system, with several vice presidents—none of whom have the longevity seen on the policy side—reporting directly to the president. As seen in figure 8, vice presidents are responsible for substantive issue areas. Currently, these are education, community development, and health. There are also several programs under a newly created vice president of research and strategic initiatives: Americorps, workforce development, leadership development, and affiliate member services.

Over the history of the organization, the programs division has fluctuated dramatically. In the 1970s, Yzaguirre and his staff obtained a number of federal grants that were used to provide technical assistance to local urban and rural groups. At the time, advocacy and policy funding was in short supply (Gallegos and O'Neill 1991). In the 1980s, when the Reagan administration pulled back funding from NCLR and many other nonprofits, NCLR struggled to stay afloat and began to seek funding from other sources. A senior staff recalls as follows the move to increase its work in policy and the resulting decline in interest at the board level in programs: "Public policy was a difficult concept to sell to the board [of directors] but then it was a huge success. We became defined by our success in public policy advocacy and lobbying. The situation changed such that our board was much more favorable to public policy, at one point seriously suggesting we quit programs entirely and just focus on public policy. This was in the early 1980s when we were having so much difficulty getting funding [for programs]."

Minutes from a 1977 board meeting reflect the preference of the board for policy activity. In that meeting, the chairman states, "The Council should concentrate on policy research and advocacy and leave the implementation of goals and program activities to the affiliates" (National Council of La Raza 1977). Interviews later in this chapter suggest that the influence of affiliates in decision-making shifts over time. The 1970s were a low period for affiliates, and board and staff appeared to be focused on their ability to influence national policy-making.

Despite funding fluctuations, and unlike the programs arm, the importance of the policy arm within the organization has been consistent from the late 1970s onward. One senior staff offers a time line marked by advocacy activity that developed NCLR's role as a player in Washington. These defining moments, this staff suggests, identified NCLR as an influential organization at the national level and within the organization affected its decision-making strategy. They also highlight the kind of work NCLR has become known for in Washington. The first marker was the 1978 Bilingual Education Act:

> That was sort of a handshake deal between Ed Roybal [member of Congress], Gus Hawkins [congressional committee chairman], and groups. It was us, MALDEF, and NABE [National Association of Bilingual Education], getting together and saying, Well, we ought to write this into a bill, and it just happened. The challenge was fairly narrow—can we get one member of Congress to make this an issue? And could he cut a deal with a committee chairman, in the days when committee chairmen were all-powerful and could do whatever they wanted? My understanding is, there wasn't even a vote. It was in the base bill.

There were several markers in the 1980s. The earliest was in 1980, when Hispanics were first counted in the national census, which provided advocates with solid numbers on which to base their claims. The Immigration Reform and Control Act of 1986 and the reauthorizations of the Bilingual Education Act were "points at which you had to make decisions about—are you going to take half a loaf, are you going to be incrementalists. . . ." With welfare reform in 1996, their strategy had clearly evolved. A senior member of staff has said, "That defined what we see as our modern lobbying strategy, which is, not just to ask people in power to do stuff with our only recourse being to criticize them or to generate heat on them (not that that's removed from our strategy, but that's the classic civil rights minority strategy), but trying to be more thoughtful about creating—can we create the landscape in which policymakers will do what we want them to do?"

As the policy arm increasingly involved itself in policy-making at the national level, programs floundered. Both board meeting minutes and comments from interview participants reveal a tension between the two pillars of the organization. One senior staff member in the programs division frankly states: "When you walk into an organization where the paradigm is 'We're the greatest, the brain trust is here' and you tell them, 'Actually, it [the brain trust] is really out in the field and not only that, but the customer is the Hispanic family,' well, that might not go over so well."

From this history we can observe that, although NCLR was heavily focused on providing assistance to community-based organizations in its early years, its focus changed not long after its move to Washington DC. As the board and leadership began to see that NCLR could play a role in national-level policy-making, its commitment to serving affiliates cooled. The time period that is the focus of this study, around 1999/2000, shows a renewed interest in the work of affiliates and in the ability of affiliates to develop viable policy alternatives. The charter school project is a dramatic example of a reversal in resources within NCLR.

By 1999, as will be detailed later, the board and organizational leadership had endorsed charter schools. At the time, the education office within the programs department at NCLR was limited in scope, with a staff of four. In a visible move to elevate this program, NCLR hired its first vice president for education, who told me, "When I first came here, my charge was, 'First, we want NCLR's [programmatic] education component to be on the map. Second, we're interested in charter schools, we think it's a good idea, can we look at that and see if we can develop something within the component.'"

As of 2004, the education programs office was staffed by twenty people and had an $8 million budget, greater than that of any other program office and far larger than that of the education office in the policy department. According to one senior staff member,

> On the program side, the investment difference is dramatic. When I started, there were three people and their jobs were to develop tools for affiliates to use—like an afterschool program that they were developing. But then we started to get involved in charter school development, and so what that meant was a large influx of funding which was matched with other dollars, so basically we went from just developing a few toolkits to a full-blown charter-school development initiative, plus these professional development institutes that were intended to give technical assistance and training to people providing direct services in charter schools, afterschools, and preschool programs. That was independent of the charter schools, but the fact that we got funding to do charter schools gave us a lot of visibility on the programmatic side which was missing up to that point. If you look at number of staff and resources, our education program staff eclipsed us [i.e., the policy side] by four or five times.

There are those within the organization, however, who believe that this renewed interest in affiliates may be short-lived. While this may be a radical view, one staff member looking forward suggests that the program side is again in decline. He argues that the charter school funding has essentially been spent, and no new funding is being developed. He suggests the programs are again stagnating:

If you look at NCLR as it is presently organized, there are no programs. The only program that is viable right now is community development. And so the only services that affiliates can get is through community development. The other programs are really small. The education money is gone; the charter school program has done what it's going to do. I don't know if it was planned that way or if it just occurred because of the funding, but there are no programs at NCLR. So you can look at it as a big downside or as an opportunity to rethink the policy/program strategy or just to admit it, we really are a policy think tank and let's just let other folks who do that well, let them do it. And just get out of that business.

Analyzing NCLR's history and structure reveals an organization that has, with the exception of financial difficulties in the 1980s, grown in size and influence. As a Hispanic organization with a Washington presence, NCLR dwarfs its sister organizations. Much of this growth has been driven by the reputation it has built through its research and advocacy work within the policy division. Its ability to fund-raise and to expand the organization has also arguably been influenced by its ideological position and its strategic approach to policy analysis and advocacy, the focus of the next section.

Ideology

Regarding NCLR's ideological position, opinions are mixed, both within and outside the organization. Within the organization, interviews revealed a resistance to defining the organization ideologically—that is, as liberal or conservative. Outside the organization, opinions of NCLR's ideology varied depending on the source. Grassroots-oriented groups tend to view NCLR as slightly more conservative, while the Washington based advocacy groups that lean to the left and Democratic members of Congress—NCLR's traditional allies—consider them to be firmly in the liberal camp. Within NCLR, one senior staff member felt it is more accurate to explain NCLR's behavior as a result of shifts along a continuum of influence: "As a general rule, the closer one is to power or the more power one has, the greater role one has in decision-making. It's also true the closer you are to power, the more often you're not going to get your way, you have to compromise, assess trade-offs. In many ways, the farther one is from power, the freer you are. To me, there are two extremes—the 'speak truth to power' extreme, and the other is to actually be the decision-maker. As the community has grown, as the organization has grown, we have moved along the continuum."

This theory has multiple implications. If this staff member is correct, then the goal-driven organization might be inclined to move closer to the decision-making end of the spectrum. However, the ideologically driven organization would prefer to maintain a position further away from power. NCLR's willingness to compromise would naturally distance NCLR from grassroots-oriented organizations whose decision-making is firmly tied to their ideological position. This approach would make it difficult for NCLR to illustrate clear victories to their grassroots; what NCLR might consider a victory, the grassroots would be more likely to consider an unacceptable compromise.

Another senior staff member objected to the idea that NCLR's ideological stance had shifted, or even that NCLR had an organizational ideology, and identified charter schools as an important indicator of this ideology-free decision-making:

> Charter schools are an outward manifestation of what we had been saying for a long time but that people didn't buy until we went out on a limb on the charter school issue. People in the education field, in the policy world, felt that we were ideologically driven, that we supported things like bilingual education because it was on the Hispanic rights agenda instead of what we had been saying all along, which was that our positions on education were always fact-driven, data-driven, and were not ideological. In fact, the question always was, What is the best way to educate our kids? At the end of the day, that's how we make every decision on education. If this proves promising for how we educate kids, we will entertain it and it doesn't matter whether conservatives support it or liberals oppose it; where it lands on the political spectrum truly is irrelevant to us if we believe it would be productive for our kids. I think charter schools was the first time we went off the reservation on an educational issue, because up until that time there was a dovetailing with a progressive educational agenda and what we believed was best for our kids.

Another senior staff member also rejects the notion of an ideologically driven NCLR, and instead labels the organization as "pragmatic." He recognizes that the result of this is a disconnect among the Hispanic advocacy groups working in Washington and the "outside groups," largely academics and regional Hispanic groups. He points to the debate surrounding bilingual education as an example. Proponents of bilingual education, who believe that teaching children in their native language is the most effective way to learn a second language, are vehemently opposed by supporters of immersion, who suggest that the quickest road to English language fluency is through complete immersion in English. Bilingual education has been traditionally supported by Democrats, while Republicans tend to support immersion. Here a staff member uses bilingual education to explain the disconnect between NCLR and other groups:

One of the things that I've seen in the last six years is we've been viewed as the most pragmatic of the Latino organizations, and sometimes that has a negative connotation outside the Beltway, but a lot of the groups inside the Beltway became pragmatic because it raises your prominence. People want to talk to you—you're at the table. All of the outside-the-Beltway groups think we sold out. But basically, there's a disconnect between the outside groups and inside groups, like we know when we went to lobby people on the Hill on bilingual education, Democrats would open the conversation by saying, 'We know bilingual education doesn't work, but we want to help you anyway'; there were *Democrats* supporting English-only legislation. The outside-the-Beltway groups don't get that. They haven't been in these conversations that are somewhat difficult with our friends. Pragmatically, if the science said tomorrow, "English immersion is the way to go," we would have to go with that—that's what the science says. Within the Beltway there's a lot of agreement because we're in the trenches dealing with policy-makers. There's a huge disagreement between us and the outside groups, because they know what the best possible situation for our kids to learn is but they don't understand that that's not going to happen.

Another perspective from senior staff, similar to that of many others interviewed, is that ideology is not a factor, but that the organization's decision-making strategy did evolve: "I wouldn't say there have been ideological changes, but there have been changes in the way we perceive things. It took us a while to change from thinking about problems to looking for opportunities. That happened in mid-1980s. We went from focusing just on our deficits to focusing on our assets as a community and began to realize that there was some danger in focusing only on being victims and not focusing on how we could take care of our own destiny."

The consistency across the interviews on the subject of ideology was surprising. NCLR's allies in Congress have traditionally and consistently been Democrats. In the interest group and advocacy group community, they have tended to be the liberal organizations. NCLR has also typically been funded by more liberal foundations and not by conservative groups. If it is true as staff suggests that this dovetailing of interests between NCLR and the progressive agenda over decades does not imply a liberal ideology, and that advocacy of charter schools is an example of its ideologically free decision-making, then NCLR is an unusual organization in the world of advocacy groups. One possible explanation is that NCLR is trying to represent all Hispanics, an increasingly diverse group politically. The other is that NCLR is driven more by its desire to participate in the policy-making process than by a strong ideological position.

Members

> It's like that MasterCard commercial, you know, fees we get
> from affiliates $100,000, relationship with affiliates, priceless.
>
> —A senior staff member

While affiliates have historically been an important part of NCLR's identity, fees from affiliates and individual members have never played a significant role in NCLR's funding. As the figure in the next section shows, membership dues account for less than 1% of NCLR's budget. This includes both individual members (who join NCLR and in return receive periodic newsletters regarding policy and advocacy activity of interest to NCLR), and affiliates, which are independent community-based organizations that receive technical assistance, access to funding, policy updates, and advocacy guidance. A senior staff member says about the role individual members play in NCLR's decision-making process: "Right now individual members are in the low thousands but very high average gifts . . . so the big group now is people giving $500 or more. And they're really heard just when they quit. Some significant number quit over our endorsement of Gonzales [for attorney general in 2005]. But there is no expectation of a role in governing. . . . Unlike Common Cause we don't have a lot of individuals donating toward policy work. . . .

This staff member suggests that portraying NCLR as a membership group uses an outdated model that does not reflect the reality of interest groups in Washington today. He suggests that organizations such as the Children's Defense Fund, Center on Budget and Policy Priorities, and Food Research and Action Center, which have no actual membership they directly represent, are much closer to NCLR's model.

Leadership interviews are not consistent with regard to the extent to which affiliates are valued and are considered influential within the organization. One senior staff member indicates that not everyone in the organization values affiliates in the same way: "When I came to NCLR, what became evident to me was that Raul Yzaguirre was a big supporter of the affiliates because he came out of that world, but the senior staff didn't really care about the affiliates. There used to be times when I used to sit there and wonder what was going on. Because that's our base and yet the comments from senior staff were, 'What's important is what we do here in Washington.' And my philosophy, coming from the grassroots, was much different."

While it does seem that the perceived role of affiliates is not consistent across the organization, affiliates do have formal opportunities to participate in decision-making. Affiliates make up one-third of the board of directors, the affiliate council is an advisory entity to the board, and regional affiliate caucuses provide an opportunity for members to provide input. Though this reflects a desire to include affiliates in the decision-making process and a call from affiliates for inclusion, interviews suggest full inclusion is still a work in progress. One board member said: "I know that Janet [Murguia, the new CEO] has been working very hard at having the affiliates be more involved. I think they do on certain issues. On the other hand, there is often a need to act rapidly, and not all the affiliates are happy about the outcomes. Great efforts are made to listen to affiliates, they're part of committees, and part of the board, but they often don't participate in many of the decisions that are made."

Another board member who is closely aligned with the affiliates suggests that in the past affiliates have felt disconnected from the work of NCLR: "As an organization that's a membership organization, you always have to find the balance between being a leader and being in tune with the community. And sometimes being a leader means taking a position that the community is not necessarily in support of. You don't want to be out there without the support of members, but at the same time I feel it's a responsibility of a leader to educate the community. . . . NCLR feels that tension."

Whether or not the formal avenues for providing input are effective, it is nevertheless true that affiliate leaders who have become influential in their own right have additional access. A senior staff member said: "I think the most prominent affiliates have always had Raul's [Yzaguirre, president of NCLR] ear; even before say Ramon Murguia was board chair, a call from him was a call I would take and be responsive to, because he knew the Kansas senators, he knew the Missouri senators, he could get a phone call returned and he would make the call. Well, geez, that's somebody we're going to be responsive to."

Ultimately, however, NCLR's goal-formation process considers the affiliate's perspective but also seeks to represent the Latino population as a whole. As one member of the staff makes clear, "We speak for the community, not for the affiliates." Another staff member elaborates: "There's also a downside to saying we represent affiliates, because we could very easily turn into a trade association, which we have not wanted to do. If we were strictly working for affiliates, we would be working on things we don't currently."

Interviews with the NCLR leadership identify issues of interest to their affiliates that NCLR did not endorse. One staff member explains how staff decides which issues to pursue: "We also do surveys and then we do policy analysis just to see if we have a shot. . . . For example, people [affiliates] talk about drivers' licenses a lot [the ability to obtain a driver's license without proof of citizenship], and we don't really push that issue very hard, because it's not an issue that we could win right now."

Interviews and evidence of decision-making on policy positions suggest that while in some cases individual affiliates may influence NCLR's policy positions, NCLR does not prioritize the direct representation of its membership, whether it is individual members or affiliates. Furthermore, NCLR's decision-making could be described as paternalistic; it uses research and a sophisticated understanding of the way Washington operates to make decisions with which the grassroots may or may not agree. While this approach has been described pejoratively by others, the present book does not seek to judge NCLR's behavior but to explain it. If NCLR prioritizes participation in policy-making, members' interests may be defined in such a way that not all members will support. In addition, NCLR's influence in Washington is based on the belief by policy-makers that NCLR represents all Hispanics, which may lead NCLR to make assumptions about the interests of Hispanics and to limit the extent to which it heeds the calls from affiliates to pursue or not pursue particular issues.

Funders

The availability of funding has significant implications for the growth and survival of a nonprofit organization. Interest group theory suggests that the extent to which funders are willing to finance particular activities affects an organization's ability to focus on issues. It has also been suggested that organizations will pursue whatever funding is available as they age, moving further away from their original ideals as they focus on survival. In the case of NCLR, while funding limitations have certainly impacted its growth in particular areas, it has also been able to foster solid reputation and relationships with funders, which has allowed it to develop its priorities as an organization without constantly worrying about fundraising and survival. As this section details, however, funding for policy has been more steadily available than for programs in recent years, and that has had implications for the growth and visibility of each division.

Over the decades, NCLR has obtained funding from the government, foundations, and the corporate sector. With the move to Washington and under the leadership of Raul Yzaguirre, the 1970s marked a period of growth for the organization. By 1980, NCLR was receiving significant dollars from the federal government in support of War on Poverty programs. However, as mentioned, actions by the Reagan administration had a severe effect on NCLR and many other social service organizations; by 1982, NCLR had lost all of its federal funding, which at the time accounted for 80% of its budget. The 1980s were a difficult time for the organization, whose very survival was threatened. Even by 1990, staff size was only fifty, half what it had been in 1980.

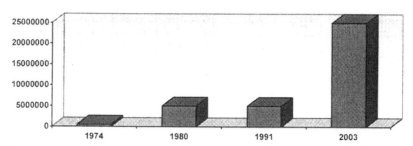

Figure 10. NCLR annual budget, 1974–2003. *Source*: National Council of La Raza 2005.

In NCLR's 2004 annual report, the memory of lean years as a result of overreliance on one funding source is evident. Current funding comes from a variety of sources, though NCLR's reliance on federal spending is somewhat higher than it would prefer. NCLR's goal is to obtain its funding equally among government, corporations, foundations, and other sources. If the memory of the 1980s was not enough, NCLR was reminded of the danger of overreliance on federal funding in 2003 when, as a result of policy positions NCLR was taking that were not in support of the Bush Administration's positions, $4 million in discretionary spending expected as part of continuing projects from several federal agencies was not disbursed (National Council of La Raza 2005). Federal funding has continued to decline; the 2006 annual report notes that as a share of budgeted revenues, federal funding declined from 20% in 2004 to 14% in 2006 (National Council of La Raza 2006).

As reliance on government spending necessarily decreased from the 1980s onward, corporate and foundation sponsors came to play a more important financial role. At the beginning of this chapter, the literature

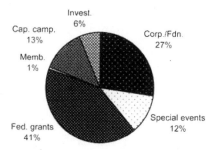

Figure 11. NCLR funding sources FY2004. *Source*: National Council of La Raza 2004.

review of Hispanic organizations found that organizations such as NCLR have been criticized for their close relationships with corporations. Ortiz suggests that their policy choices are constrained by their strategic funding strategy (1991). One member of NCLR's staff suggests that the relationships that NCLR has developed help it communicate in a more effective way with corporate interests:

> Corporations do have limited dollars, and I think we've really proven ourselves. I think we also have a national presence that resonates with corporations, as well as our thirty-year credibility. And then Janet Murguia came on board and she came from the White House. So we have a very strong presence in Washington, and the corporate world likes that. I also think that corporations appreciate our candid feedback and sometimes our direction when we start seeing that a particular corporation is having a problem with the Hispanic community. Of course, sometimes that's hard, because our roots are in civil rights, so sometimes it's difficult for some people in NCLR. But then we have opportunities, like Janet Murguia just spoke to a very exclusive meeting with CEOs around the country, where she was asked to speak about diversity. And she said to them, "It's not enough to have a recruitment program. You have to commit on a societal level from the very start. Because you won't get the candidates for top jobs that you're looking for without making a real commitment to dealing with some bigger issues, like education in the early years."

The Corporate Board of Advisors plays a significant fund-raising role. This is evidenced by the recent capital campaign, which raised $20 million dollars in eighteen months, largely from CBA members. According to this same staff member, "I think that speaks to the credibility of the institution as well as their leadership and the longevity of the relationships between these corporations and NCLR." This staff member also suggests that in addition to long-term relationships, NCLR is a good investment:

> Corporate America is committed to our institution. But understand, this is a business case for them. There was a time, prior to Enron, that a corporate CEO could say, "I really like what you're doing, here's a million dollars." They can't do that anymore. Things have to go through their foundations, their boards. And the onus is on us to tell them why a corporation should commit a con-

siderable amount of their limited philanthropy dollars to us. And so there's been a shift in the world of philanthropy. This is now about social investment. They're not just looking for a place to give their money; they're looking to make an investment. The interest is much more about how do we work with NCLR to have high-level impact that not only is a positive for the Hispanic community but is also a positive for the corporation. So we have to work harder.

As NCLR has grown and its reputation has solidified as a leader in the Hispanic community, its relationships with funders have evolved. According to another staff member, "Overall there has been a change in our funding strategy—we're now looking for people who want to invest in us. And in response to the accusation that NCLR is somehow beholden to a sponsor, I would say, 'Find one.'" Another senior staff member addresses the extent to which funders influence decision-making: "On the policy side, I think donors make almost no difference [in goal formation]. We're just so diversified. Right now I couldn't even tell you who our biggest grantor is, and it shifts from year to year."

While donors may not make specific demands on policy analysts and in the execution of programs, the CBA does appear to be interested in playing a more active role in the work of NCLR. According to a senior staff member, "The CBA does have opinions about what NCLR is doing in education. State Farm, for example, has a huge commitment to education in their giving, and they are playing a leading role in the CBA education task force." The education task force is the first time the CBA has developed a task force. This staff member explains:

> We're working with them right now on what is called the CBA educational task force, where we're taking an assessment of all the different educational programs that corporations on the CBA support, so that it not only helps corporations connect with each other in terms of what they're doing but it will also hopefully help affiliates, who will be able to see what possible corporations they can connect to without having to go through us. The task force was the idea of Jim Padilla, the chairman of the CBA and the president of the Ford Motor Company of America, and he and Janet talked about it. And it's a small project that illustrates the CBA wants to have greater engagement with us outside of financial support.

One member of staff suggests that while the organization is in a position to choose from among funders, it is also true that there are issues that are difficult to fund. Therefore NCLR is less able to pursue those avenues.

> I would argue that the funding doesn't shape our policy posi-
> tions. But funding definitely is a factor in whether we do a pro-
> gram or not or the extent to which we do a program. . . . There
> is a groupthink among the major/mainstream/left donors, and
> occasionally it is hard to break through that. So for example if
> you're in employment [working on employment policy], then
> you must be interested in extending unemployment benefits. The
> answer is, "Well, no, we're not interested in that at all, because
> half of unemployed Latino workers don't get unemployment."
> That's not easy—for a lot of center/left donors the sense is there's
> something wrong with those workers, rather than the policy.

Another problem NCLR has experienced is the response by funders when an issue becomes redefined in a way that does not correspond with their values. A staff member says: "And then the other thing [that] is more rare but still a factor is when we run up against liberal orthodoxy we have problems. Bilingual education might be one of those. First ten years it was kind of a PC [politically correct] thing, so funders said 'OK, we'll support that'; as soon as the push back came, it was 'We don't support that.'"

While financial reports from NCLR do not distinguish between funding designated for programs and funding for policy, funding difficulties may play a part in the stability of the policy pillar relative to programs. According to a staff member, the policy division has benefited from having several grants for policy generally, which allows them to fill gaps in funding as they occur. The policy division has also profited from a long-term conservative growth strategy, intended to avoid downturns and staff reductions. An important factor in this strategy is the presence within policy leadership of staff who have been with NCLR for well over a decade and who are committed to building an experienced team of policy directors and analysts. This last element is missing from the program side; leadership has cycled through, leaving little in the way of legacy.

The programs division also suffers from the financial difficulties faced by many service providers. A recent study of service providers finds funding is a major obstacle (Bridgespan Group 2005). The report, a study of twenty youth-serving organizations, found that program choices were often not strategic but were the result of a funding opportunity. It also concluded that even the larger, well-established organizations were financially fragile, often with only a few months of operating reserves. Political shifts or changes in funder preferences cause disastrous consequences. These weaknesses are characteristic of the program side of NCLR.

On the policy side, as NCLR has gained influence, it has become more able to define the problems and help funders understand issues from the Hispanic perspective. A staff member remarked: "Grant-makers tap experts in the field to inform them about how they should be spending their money and Cecilia [Munoz, vice president, Office of Research, Advocacy, and Legislation] spends a lot of time doing that, so she's helped to shape how the immigration money should be spent."

Helping funders understand the Hispanic perspective is an incremental process, which means that NCLR, while it does have considerable flexibility in choosing from among funders, is also constrained by funder preferences. A senior staff member commented: "And what that means is that some of the most important issues from the Latino community's perspective are just not—we just can't work on them. At least not to the degree we would want to. The whole workforce area is just one of those. There's just a different cut for Latinos, but it just doesn't fit with donors' ideas."

Another staff member's comment on the role of the CBA reflects the position expressed in interviews with NCLR leadership on the role of funders in decision-making: "The CBA shares their opinions, we take that in, and we make our decisions. In some cases, like we're developing an integrated marketing plan and they really have some expertise in that, so we listen. But when it comes to decisions about what NCLR will or won't do, we make those decisions on our own."

Leaders

Earlier sections described NCLR as an organization with an active volunteer board of directors and an influential cadre of paid leadership, most of whom have been with the organization for more than a decade. Board members, who are invited to join by the executive committee of the board and who are approved by the full board, establish the direction and policy priorities of the organization. They do so, however, with considerable input from staff. The CEO of the organization develops policy and programmatic goals, which are considered by the board. The board also uses staff to conduct research, develop policy positions, and provide counsel to the board based on its expertise in the policy arena. In this organization, the relationship between paid staff and volunteer board can best be described as a partnership, with staff taking an active role in bringing issues to the table for board consideration.

Conclusion

As this chapter has shown, decision-making within these leading groups is driven by very different factors. In the 1970s, as these organizations matured, they filled different roles at the national level. MALDEF was active in the courts, LULAC lobbied Congress and the administration, and NCLR provided the research to support the work of the other two groups (Zolberg 2006). Over time, this division of labor has changed. Each organization has moved in a different direction, pulled by constituencies and leadership. LULAC, much closer to the grassroots than the other groups, supports local LULAC offices but struggles to develop an agenda at the national level that incorporates research and political realities. NCLR, often criticized as being aloof and out of touch with Hispanics at the local level, uses research, analysis, and a desire to influence policy-making to guide its work at the national level. Having introduced the two organizations, the next few chapters summarize the history of education and immigration reform in the Hispanic community and apply the revised Kingdon model to goal formation on these two issues within these two organizations.

4

Education
Reform Efforts

———————————

The previous chapter provided a detailed look at two major Hispanic interest groups that work to improve the lives of Hispanics nationally. With the "who" firmly established, this chapter focuses on a few other questions: How do they pursue their goals? And what issues are at the center of their work? After a brief historical overview of advocacy in the Hispanic community, this chapter focuses on efforts to reform education policy affecting Hispanics.

A History of Advocacy

While scholars differ on where exactly the markers should be placed, several broad epochs in the history of Hispanic empowerment can be identified. Most agree that the first period begins with the Treaty of Guadalupe Hidalgo in 1848. Following the Mexican-American War, the treaty called for Mexico to cede 55% of its territory (present-day Arizona, California, New Mexico, Texas, and parts of Colorado, Nevada, and Utah) in exchange for fifteen million dollars in compensation for war-related damage to Mexican property. In this period, self-help organizations were formed, but Mexican Americans were largely disempowered by the new Anglo political hierarchy. From 1915 through the 1950s, the Mexican American middle class organized to form the League of United Latin American Citizens, and exhorted low-income Mexican Americans to behave in ways that would allow them to fit into the dominant culture (Villarreal 1988). Lopez (2001) documents the assimilationist strategy Mexican American activists pursued from the 1920s through the 1960s. According to this account, Mexican American leaders argued that Mexican Americans were racially white and therefore deserved to be treated as white people were.

By the 1960s, many leaders, feeling this strategy unsuccessful, began to follow the model of the African American civil rights movement. Though LULAC had been organized and active for decades, the "politics of protest" (Villarreal 1988) period from 1965 to 1974 is consistent with other accounts of increased activism and a birth of Chicano pride (Gonzalez 1990). In 1966, Mexican American leaders—including the LULAC leadership—walked out of an Equal Employment Commission meeting, in protest of a lack of attention to their concerns (Kaplowitz 2003). The East LA blowout of 1968 is another important benchmark of the Chicano era (Lopez 2001). In 1968, ten thousand students in East LA walked out of high schools in protest of discriminatory treatment. New leadership, disappointed by the failure of the assimilationist strategy employed by the older generation for thirty years, turned to an activist strategy that recognized Mexican Americans as separate from whites.

Finally, during the "politics of moderation and recognition" period from 1974 onward, Chicano activists from the earlier "politics of protest" period disappeared or revised their strategy, and the movement as a whole became more moderate (Villarreal 1988). Others have identified 1974 as a turn to complacency and the beginning of the end of the Chicano movement (F. C. Garcia 1988), though some recognize continued reform efforts in the Hispanic community that reflect an activist mode after 1974 (Montejano 1999).

Hispanic Education Reform Efforts

Throughout these decades of activism and moderation, a number of specific reform efforts were undertaken in the education arena with the goal of achieving equal education for Hispanics. This chapter specifically identifies four overlapping reform movements. The first sought to end education segregation. Though there is a long history of successful court cases brought by Mexican Americans, residential segregation and recent court decisions have had the effect of resegregating African Americans and Hispanics. The second, via the courts, attempted to equalize education funding. Twenty-one states have found their education systems to be unconstitutional, but only in a few cases has this translated into significant progress in equalizing funding across schools (Hunter 2006). The third pushed for the creation and adequate funding of a federal bilingual education program. Bilingual education, while enacted and funded at the federal level, has been eliminated in many states and is highly controversial. The fourth has centered on charter schools, and is in several ways different from earlier reform movements. The charter school movement is a departure from earlier Hispanic education reform efforts in that many Hispanic community-based organizations embraced a movement that was not initially endorsed by the national Hispanic organizations.

Desegregation, school finance, and bilingual education are defined by national and community-based activism working in tandem and aimed at the existing school system; they chiefly call for equal and appropriate treatment of Hispanic students. The Hispanic-led charter school movement is a groundswell from Hispanic grassroots organizations that, despite a neutral or oppositional stance toward charters at the national Hispanic level, decided that starting charter schools would empower the Hispanic community in a way not possible in the traditional public school system.

Segregation and Desegregation

The story of school segregation of Hispanics is largely about Mexican Americans in the late nineteenth and early twentieth centuries, before other Hispanics made up a significant part of the Hispanic population. More recently, other Hispanic groups have been similarly segregated and have pressed for reform. For decades following the 1848 Treaty of Guadalupe Hidalgo, segregated schools were the norm in Southwest states, despite the absence of any laws on record that permitted the segregation of students based on their Mexican heritage (Bowman 2001). Survey research from the 1930s finds that 85% of schools in California segregated Mexican Americans (Valencia 2002). Schools were similarly segregated in Texas; research found 90% of Texas schools racially segregated (Valencia 2002). This practice was often justified on the grounds that Mexicans were unclean, had learning difficulties that could disrupt the academic progress of white students, and had language problems (Donato 1997). In segregated schools, Americanization programs prepared Mexican children for vocational work (Bernal 2000). In many cities, only the lower schools were segregated; dropout rates were sufficiently high to make segregation of high schools unnecessary (Valencia 2002). Mexican Americans sought redress in the courts; several cases were successful and marked the beginning of the fight against segregated schooling.

INDEPENDENT SCHOOL DISTRICT V. SALVATIERRA (1930)

The first of many legal battles to end segregation was led by LULAC (Valencia 2002). With support from LULAC, parents in Del Rio, Texas, brought *Independent School District v. Salvatierra* (1930) when the school board made known their plans to increase the segregation of Mexican students (Bowman 2001). The district court ruled in favor of the plaintiffs, and found that the school district had illegally segregated Mexican American students based on race (1930). However, the Texas Court of Civil Appeals overturned the district court's decision and decided that the school district was not actively segregating in a discriminatory manner; rather, the schools separated the Mexican American children because they started the school year late due to their work in the fields, and were as a result academically behind the white students. They also justified the separation of students on the basis of language differences. These benign reasons for dividing Mexican Americans from others would be used to continue to segregate children for several decades (G. A. Martinez 1994). The case is an excellent example of the arbitrary nature of court decisions; despite the fact that white children who entered school after the year had begun were not sent to the Mexican school, the district was allowed to segregate Mexican Americans for that reason. In fact, it is clear that the Mexican Americans were segregated based on their nationality. Evidence of the belief at the time that Mexican Americans were physically different from white children can be found in the statement of the superintendent in the case: "I have been told that it is true that a Mexican child will reach the puberty stage sooner than an American child, and that people originating in torrid climates will mature earlier, owing to the climactic conditions" (*Independent School District et al v. Salvatierra et al*).

ALVAREZ V. LEMON GROVE (1931)

In what has been called the nation's first successful desegregation court case (Donato 1997), but also an anomaly in the early history of Mexican American desegregation cases, a group of parents in a small town in California surprised the town's white leadership by resisting efforts to segregate their children (Alvarez 1988). Participating in a rising tide of anti-Mexican sentiment, the school board of Lemon Grove had, behind closed doors, decided to move the seventy-five Mexican American students attending the Lemon Grove Grammar School to a separate building. Parents of the Mexican American students rallied; with the support of LULAC, they retained counsel and demanded equal treatment for their children (Cockcroft 1994). The court ruled that the school board did not have the right to separate the children based on their country of origin. However, the Lemon Grove case was not used as a precedent for opposing segregated schools in other California cities (Alvarez 1988).

MENDEZ V. WESTMINSTER (1946)

Mendez is known as the most significant court case affecting the de jure segregation of Mexican children in the Southwest (Bowman 2001). The case was brought by five Mexican American parents in Orange County, California, on behalf of their children and five thousand other Mexican American children in the surrounding counties who attended segregated schools (Robinson and Robinson 2003). Supported by LULAC, they argued that segregation violated the due process and equal protection clauses of the Fourteenth Amendment to the United States Constitution (Bowman

2001). *Mendez* has been recognized as a precursor to *Brown v. Board of Education*, as the decision was a clear departure from the "separate but equal" doctrine of *Plessy v. Ferguson* (1896) (Valencia 2002). In the lower court ruling, in finding for the plaintiffs the judge noted that the students were not in fact segregated due to language ability but based on their surnames or appearance (Robinson and Robinson 2003). The Ninth Circuit Court upheld the lower court's ruling in 1947. The case was considered by many minority advocates as a critical step toward desegregation, as witnessed by the amicus curiae briefs submitted by groups representing African Americans, Japanese Americans, and the American Jewish Congress (Robinson and Robinson 2003). The decision had immediate repercussions; within weeks LULAC filed *Delgado v. Bastrop Independent School District* (1948) in Texas, which successfully ended state-mandated segregation. Legislative victories at the state level also followed in California.

REFORM IN THE POST-*BROWN* ERA

In *Brown v. Board of Education*, the Supreme Court unanimously decided that "[s]egregation of white and Negro children in the public schools of a State solely on the basis of race, pursuant to state laws permitting or requiring such segregation, denies to Negro children the equal protection of the laws guaranteed by the Fourteenth Amendment—even though the physical facilities and other 'tangible' factors of white and Negro schools may be equal" (347 U.S. 483 [1954]).

While this marked the beginning of the civil rights revolution for African Americans (Orfield and Yun 1999), Mexican Americans were slow to embrace the constitutional substance of *Brown* (Wilson 2003). Rather they continued to rely on a separate canon, which argued that Mexican Americans were white, and disregarded *Brown*'s usefulness. Lawyers employing this "other" canon often called for better policing of the existing boundaries of Jim Crow, rather than the dismantling of the system; they argued that their cases were about the denial of due process rather than a denial of equal rights. This "other white" strategy would not be abandoned for fifteen years after *Brown*.

By the late 1960s, the limited benefits of "due process" victories did not justify the investment. Instead of expending their energy in the courts, Mexican Americans in those intervening years sought to expand their political power (Villarreal et al. 1988). As a result of this push, Hispanics were appointed to judgeships and won elections in municipalities and in the Congress. LULAC pressed at the local and national level for more appointments of Mexican Americans to critical government positions. However, their continued embrace of "white" status prevented Mexican Americans from grappling with the practical distinction between the de jure segregation of African Americans that the Supreme Court had condemned in *Brown* and the de facto segregation experienced by Hispanics. Militants of the new political generation were less willing to accept the "white" label, given the reality of segregation. In 1967, the Ford Foundation invested $2.2 million in creating a new organization, MALDEF, which was modeled after NAACP's legal defense fund. By 1975, MALDEF suits had led to the desegregation and provision of bilingual and bicultural programs in ten school districts, and had ended discriminatory testing practices that resulted in Mexican American students being inappropriately placed in special education (Ford Foundation 1975). MALDEF filed the pathbreaking lawsuit in Corpus Christi that argued that *Brown* should apply to Mexican Americans (Wilson 2003).

CISNEROS V. CORPUS CHRISTI INDEPENDENT SCHOOL DISTRICT (1971)

In *Cisneros v. Corpus Christi Independent School District* (1971), the judge ruled that Mexicans could not be paired with African Americans in order to meet desegregation requirements, but that Mexicans were an identifiable minority group and therefore entitled to the protection provided under *Brown* (Valencia 2002). The case also marks a change in the legal strategy of Hispanics in segregation cases. After *Cisneros*, plaintiffs sought to be identified as a minority group, rather than as "other white," as had been the strategy in the decades before *Brown* (Valencia 2002). The *Keyes v. Denver* (1973) case confirmed this development.

KEYES V. DENVER (1973)

Despite many cases in local and state courts, it was not until 1973 in *Keyes v. Denver School District No. 1* that the U.S. Supreme Court heard a Mexican American desegregation case and recognized that educational discrimination against Hispanics must be considered in suits to desegregate public education (Meier and Stewart 1991). Despite earlier victories, including the *Mendez* case, it is not until *Cisneros* and *Keyes* that Latino students were considered "nonwhite" and therefore should be classified with African American students for the purposes of desegregation. After twenty years, the *Brown v. Board of Education* decision, known to all as the landmark desegregation case, was applied to Hispanics (Bowman 2001).

CONCLUSION

This review has confirmed that Hispanics—parents, local organizations, and national groups—have organized at the grassroots level, marshaled resources, rallied public opinion, and brought many cases to the courts in an effort to end segregation practices in public schools. It would be decades after the *Brown* decision before Hispanics changed their approach from pursuing a strategy that set them apart from African American reformers to one that recognized Hispanics as a separate class from whites. Despite legal victories, segregation has continued across the country. The courts moved from allowing segregation based on benign factors to justifying segregation on the grounds that segregation was not the result of state action, but due to forces outside the control of the courts (G. A. Martinez 1994). Over time, as de jure segregation disappeared, de facto segregation persisted. Despite the existence of residential segregation, courts have lifted desegregation orders in at least three dozen school districts in the last ten years. These lower courts responded to a Supreme Court decision that considered schools to be desegregated even if imbalances due to residential segregation existed. Consequently, Hispanics are now more segregated than ever before; Latino students now attend schools where whites account for only 29% of all students, compared to 45% three decades ago (Frankenberg et al. 2003).

In addition to their efforts to integrate schools, Hispanic civil rights activists have also turned directly to the issue of equalizing school finance through the courts.

School Finance Reform

The second movement was premised on the notion that inequitable funding significantly impacts the quality of education Hispanics and other minorities receive. While black and Hispanic advocates have been pressing the federal government to end discrimination based on race, advocates have for the past thirty years also charged in state courts that schools are segregated by resources, with some schools in districts with high property values receiving much higher levels of financing than other schools situated in poor areas. Even as civil rights lawyers have continued to work for desegregation in schools, they have also recognized that regardless of the racial profile of a school, the level of funding that school receives is critical (Reed 2001).

The first school finance lawsuits arose in California, Texas, and New Jersey. Several of the first major court cases challenging the constitutionality of education finance systems were brought by Hispanic parents hoping to equalize spending across wealthy suburban districts and poor Hispanic urban districts. The first such case was *Serrano v. Priest*, which was filed by Hispanic parents in California.

Serrano v. Priest (1971)

In two major decisions, *Serrano I* (1971) and *Serrano II* (1976), the California Supreme Court declared California's property-tax-based school-finance system to be unconstitutional and a violation of equal protection principles. In response, the California legislature devised a funding formula that would equalize funding to within a $200 maximum difference in per-pupil spending. While this mechanism, which created a state-level pool of funds from local revenues that was then redistributed equally among districts, was technically successful, *Serrano* also had some serious unintended consequences. As a result of *Serrano* and the loss of control over local spending on schools, a taxpayer revolt led to the passage of Proposition 13, which in turn had the effect of lowering per-pupil spending in California dramatically (Fischel 1996).

Proposition 13 decreased local tax revenues by 60% by limiting the property tax rate to 1% of the assessed property value and holding annual increases to 2%; it also provided that any new tax increases must be approved by a two-thirds majority of voters (Fischel 1996; Trifiletti 2004). Voter approval of an increase was not likely, given that particular school districts would not see significant spending increases as a result of increases in taxes. Per-pupil spending in California, as a result, has been among the lowest in the nation.

In addition, the *Serrano* decisions capped per-pupil revenues in high-spending districts in order to equalize school spending. However, the court had overlooked the fact that 75% of poor children lived in high-spending districts such as San Francisco and Oakland. Thus, the *Serrano* decisions actually led to lower school spending for many poor children. While the unintended consequences of *Serrano* were disastrous, civil rights groups recognized that the California Supreme Court had found the California school system unconstitutional, and the case encouraged parents in other states to take similar action (Odden and Picus 2000).

RODRIGUEZ V. SAN ANTONIO (1971)

Rodriguez v. San Antonio, filed in Texas only a few months after the first *Serrano* decision, would be a critical case in the history of school-finance litigation. In 1968, four hundred Mexican American students at Edgewood High School in San Antonio staged a walkout in protest of inequitable funding at their school and in their school district. In Texas, due largely to unequal tax bases, spending per student varied across districts from a low of $2,112 to a high of $19,333 (Yarab 1990). The walkout led to the formation of the Edgewood District Concerned Parents Association and, with some assistance from LULAC, to the filing of the *Rodriguez* case on behalf of poor Texas schoolchildren who resided in districts with low property-tax bases (Orozco 1996).

The plaintiffs challenged the structure of school financing, which was partially based on property taxes, as unconstitutional under the Fourteenth Amendment. The plaintiffs asked that the provision of education be recognized as a fundamental right, which would require a more careful assessment of wealth-based discrimination in education (Reed 2001). The three-judge court ruled on *Rodríguez* in December 23, 1971. The panel held the Texas school-finance system unconstitutional under the equal protection clause of the Fourteenth Amendment. The state appealed, and the case went to the United States Supreme Court as *San Antonio Independent School District v. Rodríguez*. On March 21, 1973, the Supreme Court ruled five to four against Rodríguez, stating that the system of school finance did not violate the U.S. Constitution and that the issue should be resolved by the state of Texas. The court rejected the notion of education as a fundamental right, and that the Fourteenth Amendment's equal protection clause requires the court to consider poverty as a suspect classification (Reed 2001). While on its face a negative outcome, some have argued that the Supreme Court decision was the spark the led to court cases in states across the country: "*Rodriguez*, when you look at it closely, laid out the challenge. The challenge is proving that money really matters and that courts can be effective in rectifying the problem" (Rebell 1998). Over the next thirty years, perhaps as a result of the *Rodriguez* decision, forty-five states have found themselves facing school financing lawsuits, with half of the suits resulting in an overturning of the existing funding system. Texas was one such state.

EDGEWOOD INDEPENDENT SCHOOL DISTRICT V. KIRBY

The Mexican American Legal Defense and Educational Fund filed *Edgewood Independent School District v. Kirby* against commissioner of education William Kirby on May 23, 1984, in Travis County on behalf of the Edgewood Independent School District, San Antonio, citing discrimination against students in poor school districts. The Edgewood school district, sixty-seven other school districts, and parents and children who were represented in the suit argued that the school financing system violated the Texas constitution. The trial court agreed, the court of appeals reversed the trial court decision, and, in 1989, the Texas Supreme Court affirmed the trial court's decision and overturned the entire school system (Yarab 1990). After several legislative attempts and related court cases, in 1995 the legislature finally developed a plan to redistribute funds from the wealthiest districts to the poorest districts. In 2004, in response to continued inequities in the system, MALDEF and others again went to the courts charging continued inequities in school finance. In *West Orange-Cove Consolidated ISD v. Nelson*, the court ruled in their favor, finding that the demonstrated inequities rendered the school finance system inefficient, in violation of Article VII, Section 1 of the Texas constitution.

Conclusion

In California and Texas, the school finance systems were overturned as a result of court cases initially brought by Hispanic parents. As of 2006, there have been twenty-one plaintiff victories and seven state defendant victories with nine cases pending (Hunter 2006). In those states where education systems have been found unconstitutional, protracted litigation has typically ensued. Litigation in New Jersey spans three decades; similarly, *Serrano v. Priest* (1971) in California is still being debated (Walter et al. 2003). Though there have been court victories, research shows the political obstacles to implementing reform are significant, and comprehensive change is not likely to come easily, even with a favorable court decision (Carr and Fuhrman 1999).

Bilingual Education

Bilingual education, contrary to popular wisdom, is not the product of 1960s civil rights reform. Bilingual education is rooted in the first immigrant communities from Germany and France. These communities established schools and provided instruction in their native language (Ryan 2002). This activity was often met with the same antipathy found in the modern-day English-only movement. For example, Benjamin Franklin's papers reveal a fear that Germans might overwhelm English-speakers in Pennsylvania: "Why should the Palatine Boors be suffered to swarm into our Settlements, and by herding together, establish their language and Manners, to the Exclusion of ours?" (Franklin 1961; Crawford 2000).

Bilingual education was not, however, a topic around which Mexican Americans in the early 1900s mobilized. LULAC and the American GI Forum, the first national Hispanic organizations, stressed social, political, and economic justice and attempted to integrate into American life (Donato 1997). They supported bilingual education only to the extent that it facilitated assimilation (Kaplowitz 2003). Bilingual education, therefore, did not become a popular remedy in the Hispanic community until after activists in the 1960s asserted a position of ethnic pride (Crawford 2000). Bilingual education also gained political support as an alternate remedy to address the needs of limited-English-proficient (LEP) students. The Civil Rights Act of 1964 provided the basis for future court cases:

> Sec. 2000d. Prohibition against exclusion from participation in, denial of benefits of, and discrimination under federally assisted programs on ground of race, color, or national origin:
>
> No person in the United States shall, on the ground of race, color, or national origin, be excluded from participation in, be

denied the benefits of, or be subjected to discrimination under any program or activity receiving Federal financial assistance. (Pub. L. 88-352, title 6, sec. 601, *Stat.* 78 [July 2, 1964]: 252)

In 1968, President Lyndon Johnson signed into law the Bilingual Education Act as an addendum to Title VII of the Elementary and Secondary Education Act. The intent of the legislation was to redress historical evidence of discrimination against school-aged students whose language differed from English. In particular, the Bilingual Education Act provided financial aid to school districts developing innovative programs that addressed the special needs of low-income minority students (Becerra 1995).

Lau v. Nichols (1974)

In 1974, a lawsuit brought by Chinese parents in San Francisco led to a Supreme Court ruling that *identical* education does not constitute *equal* education under the Civil Rights Act. The court's decision in the landmark *Lau v. Nichols* case required schools to take "affirmative steps" to overcome language barriers impeding children's access to the curriculum. In the same year, Congress passed the Equal Educational Opportunity Act, extending the *Lau* decision to all schools. As *Lau* remedies and court orders were imposed on schools, a backlash was born that led to a fierce debate over the efficacy of bilingual education programs that continues today (Crawford 2000).

Serna v. Portales (1974)

Following *Lau*, MALDEF filed *Serna v. Portales*. In 1974 the Tenth Circuit Court of Appeals found that the achievement levels of Spanish-surnamed students were below those of their Anglo counterparts. The court ordered Portales Municipal Schools to implement a bilingual/bicultural curriculum, revise procedures for assessing achievement, and hire bilingual school personnel.

Castañeda v. Pickard (1981)

In responding to the plaintiffs' claim that Raymondville, Texas Independent School District's language remediation programs violated the Equal Educational Opportunities Act of 1974, the Fifth Circuit Court of Appeals formulated a set of basic standards to determine school district compliance with the act (Sosa 1994). The "Castañeda test" includes the following criteria: (1) theory—the school must pursue a program based on an educational theory recognized as sound or, at least, as a legitimate experimental strategy; (2) practice—the school must actually implement the program with instructional practices, resources, and personnel necessary to transfer theory to reality; and (3) results—the school must not persist in a program that fails to produce results.

English Only

Despite apparent victories in the courts, bilingual education has been a major source of controversy, pitting those who believe bilingual education helps children learn English without losing their first language against those who believe Americans should speak "English only." The enactment of Proposition 227 in California marked a decided turn in the tide against bilingual education. Proponents of making English the official language had been pursuing their goals at the national level since 1981, when Senator S. I. Hayakawa began introducing proposals to amend the Constitution to declare English the official language of the United States. Unsuccessful in his attempts in Congress, he founded the organization U.S. English. Ron Unz headed the California chapter of U.S. English that spearheaded Proposition 227. It mandated English immersion to be used for the state's English-learner population. The measure was approved by 61% of the California electorate in June 1998. This proposition eliminates bilingual education and replaces it with participation for one year in a "sheltered English" classroom, followed by immersion in English-only classrooms. It also allows parents to sue teachers who do not engage in English-only instruction. By 1999 Ron Unz had funded a poll that found an overwhelming majority of New Yorkers prefer English immersion (Tierney 1999). By 2001, a similar proposition passed in Arizona with 63% of the vote (Moran 1987; Ryan 2002). As of 2008, twenty-eight states have adopted some form of law making English the official language.

Conclusion

English-only proponents argue that even Hispanic parents want their children to be in intensive one-year immersion programs, rather than in bilingual education (Tierney 1999). Advocates for bilingual education argue that funding for bilingual education has never been adequate to serve current limited-English-proficient students and, as the number of LEP students grows, funding falls further behind (Committee for Education Funding 2003). In California, prior to the implementation of Proposition 227, only 30% of LEP students were enrolled in bilingual education taught in their native language (Bangs 1999). Inadequate funding of this program, according to advocates, also has serious implications for local districts and states, given the significant new accountability and reporting requirements for LEP students in the No Child Left Behind law (NABE 2003). In addition, the English-only reformers have been criticized for taking decision-making authority away from local educators (Moran 1987; Bangs 1999)

In summary, despite court decisions, enacted programs, and research that shows that learning a new language is facilitated by native-language instruction, anti-immigrant sentiment and strong assimilationist attitudes across the nation, particularly in states with large immigrant populations, have severely hampered the implementation of bilingual education (Crawford 2000; Ovando 2003).

Charter Schools

In 1991, Minnesota enacted the first charter school law in the country. Other states quickly followed, and by 1992 Bill Clinton, then the Democratic candidate for president, had endorsed the charter school concept. By 1994, the federal government included funding for charter schools in the Elementary and Secondary Education Act reauthorization. By 2000, more spending for charter schools was on the agendas of both major presidential candidates. The Bill and Melinda Gates Foundation began providing significant funding to charters, and in 2002, the No Child Left Behind Act provided $300 million in funding for charter schools. In 2005, there were approximately 3,400 charter schools operating in forty states, serving one million students, or 2% of students in public schools (Vanourek 2005). By 2007, the National Alliance for Public Charter Schools counted 4,046 schools serving 1.1 million students (see www.publiccharters.org).

As in any policy debate, there are champions and detractors. The champions consider charters the laboratories of innovation, freed from the shackles of public school bureaucracy. Charters provide parents with the ability to choose the school they feel best serves their children. Charters allow teachers flexibility to design curriculum that is tailored to the needs of their classrooms. Critics, including labor and public school administrators, point to reports that suggest charter schools are not serving students any better than the public school system (Wells 2002). They say there is no accountability and that charters will lead to further segregation—some say balkanization—of society (Cooper 2002).

In the early years of the charter school movement, citizens were concerned that charter schools would be used by suburban middle- and upper-class parents in lieu of private schools. Historically, in fact, "choice" was used as a mechanism to resist desegregation efforts in the South; white parents sent their children to private schools in order to avoid sending their children to racially mixed public schools (Henig 1996).

In 1990, *Politics, Markets & America's Schools* outlined a model of choice that garnered a great deal of attention (Chubb and Moe 1990; Fuller 2000; Marquez 2003). While the choice plan offered by Chubb and Moe was a voucher plan, the concerns raised by minority activists in response to their proposal would flavor much of the later debates on charter schools. In fact, the case studies in the next chapter find a frequent conjoining of vouchers and charters by those opposed to charter schools, despite the many differences between the two models of choice.

The Chubb and Moe plan would have required that schools make admissions decisions, in order to ensure that their target population would actually be the group served. This would have immediately raised a concern among minority advocates that harder-to-serve students would not be targeted—private schools in a voucher system and charters would just "cream" the best students from the public schools (Benveniste et al. 2003). Chubb and Moe suggest that the harder-to-serve students would come with larger scholarships, so that schools would be eager to enroll them. However, regardless of the size of the scholarships, the danger is that schools will want students who can show results quickly. In an age of accountability, their model had no accountability other than the market, which they argued would be enough.

Minority advocates also worried that unequal access to information would leave some children in schools that have been depleted by the departure of more-able students with more-involved parents (Tweedie et al. 1990). This was an argument that would continue to be made with regard to charter schools. It was argued that parents with less education and income and racial minorities would not have the same access to information and would not have the ability to make educational decisions (Levin 1990).

Proponents of market-based reform fueled anxiety about creaming and taking money from the system where most minorities will be—that is, in the traditional public school system, which could become a dumping ground for students who might be more expensive or harder to serve. The choice movement was enthusiastically adopted by the Republican Party; states with early charter school laws were led by Republicans, and libertarians such as Charles Murray eagerly endorsed charter schools as a second-best alternative to vouchers, which would remove government from the provision of education entirely (Murray 1997). In the Hispanic community, and certainly at the national level, the response to charter schools was largely negative. While Hispanics are politically diverse, much of the national leadership in Washington-based Hispanic organizations relate more directly to the Democratic Party, dating back to the civil rights movement.

Several recent books on Hispanic education have made what are, at best, guarded statements on charter schools. With regard to charter schools as an alternative, a chapter in Valencia 2003 on segregation warns that, looking at choice in Denver, only white parents tend to have the economic means to choose schools when transportation is not provided. This chapter also suggests that charter schools should be subject to desegregation requirements and warns that "charters are more likely to further individual aspiration than lead to generalized improvement in public schools, and thus, charters, like vouchers, reinforce a two-tiered society" (Valencia 2002, 230). Kloosterman 2003, another book that provides an overview of Hispanic education, makes only a passing reference to charter schools. Bartolome's chapter in the Kloosterman book devotes one paragraph to the phenomenon; she mentions NCLR's charter school project but suggests that there is little evidence that charters are having a clearly positive influence on outcomes (Bartolome 2003).

Research does not confirm the fears that Hispanics would not be served by charter schools. Minorities are just over half of the population served in the charter school system; whites make up less than half (U.S. Department of Education 2002). Furthermore, the systems each serve approximately the same percentage of school lunch recipients and children who are limited-English-proficient. This suggests that, contrary to early concerns about unequal parental education and resources, parents of all races and incomes have made the decision to move their children to a charter school. In addition, while the definitive answer is not yet available, Brian Gill (2001) makes an interesting point about the difficulty of understanding the effects on integration based on district-level data. First, charters may improve integration if white students who had been in exclusive white private schools come back to the public school system, even if they are still a majority at the school. Second, charters, which are smaller, are less likely to have tracking. It is possible then that a charter school with the same racial/ethnic breakdown as the local traditional school might be more integrated within the school.

As to the efficacy of charter schools, the data to date is mixed (Angostini 2003; Dillon and Schemo 2004; Viadero 2004; Viadero 2004; Hassel et al. 2007). While evaluations have found that charter schools do not serve minorities as well or do not score as well as traditional schools, those reports have been criticized for not looking at scores over time or for considering the harder-to-serve populations in charter schools. A recent meta-analysis of charter school achievement for low-income students found two studies that suggest economically disadvantaged students do worse in charter schools, four studies that find they do better, and two studies that find no significant difference between public and charter schools (Hassel 2005).

CHARTER SCHOOLS ON THE HISPANIC EDUCATION AGENDA

For decades, the major national civil rights organizations have sought to institutionalize the goals of the equity agenda. MALDEF and others have actively filed suits on behalf of bilingual education programs and challenging discriminatory admissions practices and school financing systems. There exists a national bilingual education program, renamed English Language Acquisition, which was funded at $676 million in 2005. The high school completion rate for Hispanics has improved over time. There have been victories—in particular battles, at least. But while a slightly larger percentage of Hispanics are completing high school now than in past decades (up to 64.1% in 2000 from 56.2% in 1972), the gap between Hispanics and non-Hispanics shows no sign of shrinking (U.S. Department of Education 2003). Given the intense activity on the part of community-based organizations in providing afterschool supports and participating in multiple ways in efforts to change the educational opportunities afforded to Hispanics within the current system, it seems a logical next step to start schools that are specifically designed to serve the Hispanic community. In fact, some of the oldest Hispanic community-based organizations began as alternative schools, created to fill a void in communities where the education system was not effectively meeting the needs of Hispanics (Kloosterman 2003). This is particularly true of certain subgroups, such as limited-English speakers and migrant farmworker youth. The community-based organizations were often the only provider in the community serving that group's needs (Orum 1984).

Funding these schools has always been complicated; since they serve low-income populations, parents are not able to contribute financially. Instead, alternative schools have relied on funding cobbled together from state and federal programs, contractual relationships with the local districts, and cooperative agreements with local businesses (Orum 1984). The advent of the charter school movement provided an opportunity to obtain per-pupil funding, sometimes on par with that of the traditional public schools. The charter school movement also supplied the impetus to many organizations to move from an afterschool program to a full-fledged school serving a group of students with particular needs.

CONCLUSION

This section finds that Hispanic-led charter schools are a recent addition to the larger education agenda in the Hispanic community. Considering several variables critical to each of the reform movements, Hispanic-led charter schools are in several ways different from previous reform efforts.

First, while a division between whites and different minority aggregations characterized other movements, the range of racial/ethnic groups embraces the charter school movement. Second, Hispanic-led charter schools do not pose a threat to more-affluent and white parents, which is a stumbling block for the three earlier movements. Although one argument against charter schools is that they drain money from the public school systems, it may be that Hispanic-led charter schools are welcomed because they reach a population that the public school system finds hard to serve. Third, while earlier movements ultimately pitted different ideological groups against one another, the charter school movement was expanded to allow for a wide range of ideas. The early charter school movement was not concerned with multiracial issues; however, as Kingdon (1984) points out, policies are often pushed by policy entrepreneurs who are willing to attach their "solution" to other problems in order to be more politically viable. This partially explains why new coalitions emerge around policies like charter schools. Fourth, in all the movements the reforms were successful at the institutional level—laws were passed or programs were put in place. However, while the other reforms struggle, the charter school movement is growing; in 2005 the number of charter schools grew by 13% (Allen 2005). Funding for Hispanic-serving charters is more readily available at the federal level and from foundations, and some national organizations, including NCLR, are providing technical support so that the schools can assess their students' progress and develop appropriate programs to meet their needs. Of course, a positive prognosis assumes outcomes from Hispanic-led charter schools will be better than in the current system; that research has not yet been done. Finally, the charter school movement in the Hispanic community emerges from the local level; parents and community-based organizations largely support the concept. Unlike other issues on which the local and national groups agree, in this case it was the local groups that compelled at least NCLR, if not other national groups, to examine and adjust its position on charter schools.

Conclusion

Hispanic advocates have long recognized the importance of education as a means of improving the socioeconomic status of Hispanics. Parents, students, community organizations, and national advocacy organizations have for decades demanded an equal education for Hispanic children. There has been progress; de jure segregation no longer exists, bilingual education has been federally funded for decades, and the civil rights movement has forever changed definitions of equality. However, de facto segregation persists, and Hispanic educational achievement lags considerably behind white and black educational attainment. Structural and school-based impediments have not been easily remedied, and the prognosis is not good for future success on these fronts.

Having provided the context in which Hispanic advocates operate, the next chapter carefully details the reactions of two leading national Hispanic civil rights organizations to the charter school movement. As this chapter will show, NCLR and LULAC did not follow the same path. The rationale of these organizations in pursuing some policy alternatives and not others should provide a deeper understanding of why these organizations have pursued the policy alternatives they have, and also may help us predict what the future holds for Hispanic reform efforts.

5

Goal Formation on Charter Schools

The response to charter schools by NCLR and LULAC could not have been more different. NCLR endorsed the concept of charter schools and created a program to support affiliates who had started or wanted to start charter schools. LULAC has never supported charter schools, instead arguing for increased attention and spending on the traditional public school system. This chapter first provides an account of NCLR's goal-formation process on this issue and then turns to LULAC. With an understanding of these organizations' histories and a general understanding of their goal-formation process from the previous chapters, the application of the revised Kindgon model to the charter school case should clarify the importance of funders, members, and leaders, and will test the utility of the Kingdon streams in the study of interest groups.

NCLR's Response to Charter Schools

Having explored the history of NCLR, the varied opinions regarding their ideology, their decision-making strategy, and the roles of members, funders, and leaders, I now turn to a particular point in time that is an important marker in the organization's development and for the Hispanic education agenda. NCLR's critics charged that their acceptance of charter schools is a perfect example of its strategy of accommodation. Those opposed to charter schools suggest they allow privileged groups to exit the public system, leaving public schools underresourced. Even if Hispanics are represented in the charter school population, most Hispanics will continue in public schools. Support for charter schools, therefore, undermines the goal of improving educational outcomes for all Hispanic students. Why did NCLR take this path and what does this suggest about its education agenda?

In this chapter, it is evident that the three groups that have been identified by interest group theorists as important to the goal-formation process—
members, funders, and leaders—play important roles within NCLR and
in the debate over charter schools. The need to maintain diverse funding
sources, constraints imposed by funders, the needs and the capacity of affiliates, and the opinions of key leaders are all factors, though in varying
degrees. One senior staff at NCLR shared the internal calculus used in its
goal-formation process. Now codified across the organization, there are
four basic questions:

> One is need/impact; how many people are affected and how se-
> verely they are affected. Second is an added value question. What is
> our capacity to make a difference, to what extent are we uniquely
> positioned to make a difference? And then the third factor is sort of
> an institutional consideration (we'll look at questions of geogra-
> phy): Is this an area where we want to expand? We're really inter-
> ested in building a larger footprint in California, so we're going to
> be looking at stuff there—so institutional interests are important.
> Fourth are the stakeholder interests. . . . [T]he classic question is a
> federal budget question—there's one line item in the budget that
> serves, say, family day care, which is very important to Latinos, but
> fairly moderate to minimal affiliate involvement—versus Head
> Start appropriations, which affiliates are really involved in. We're
> going to work more on what the affiliates are involved in.

The analysis of the charter school issue that follows finds that the factors that this staff member, an especially acute internal observer, offers,
while helpful, do not entirely explain the endorsement of charter schools or
the scope of the program that developed as a result. After charting the path
of charter school endorsement, I apply the goal-formation framework introduced in chapter 1 to explain the adoption of charter schools by NCLR.

Endorsing Charter Schools

> A truly bizarre set of political bedfellows now pushes to expand
> charter schools and widen school options in general.
>
> —B. Fuller

Early proponents of school choice, seeing an opportunity to expand their
base of support, moved from promoting a market remedy that would
provide choice to largely affluent communities to an opportunity for poor
people to take control of their children's education (Fuller 2000). While
national Hispanic organizations continued to be wary of any reforms
that would draw money away from more universal concerns, such as

inequities in school finance, the previous chapter showed how some local groups, parents, and community leaders saw charter schools as an opportunity that could not be ignored.

NCLR, however, maintained a neutral position on charters for nearly a decade after the first state-approved charter schools. It was not until 1999 that the NCLR board of directors adopted a position on charter schools, which was as follows:

> NCLR reaffirms its support for a strong, stable public school system charged with the responsibility of providing a high-quality education to all students. NCLR supports the establishment and strengthening of community-based charter schools, particularly those designed to serve Latino and other children who may be at-risk of school failure, as long as such schools: have adequate and safe facilities; provide a high-quality education that is fully accredited; fully comply with civil rights, special education, and other requirements, as appropriate; and assure that Hispanic parents have all the information necessary to make informed decisions regarding participation. (NCLR 1999)

After their endorsement, NCLR launched a highly publicized national campaign to support their affiliates who were starting charter schools. By 2000, NCLR announced it had raised $6.7 million to develop a network of Latino-oriented charter schools. By 2001, NCLR launched the Charter School Development Initiative. The program's goal was to build and improve fifty Latino community-based charter schools in five years. By 2002, NCLR had met their fund-raising goal of $10 million for the initiative and had awarded twenty-six grants to schools in ten states. By 2004, the initiative included eighty charter schools serving twenty thousand Latino students.

Goal Formation and Charter Schools

> Most of our policies are either reactive or top-down driven, so this was unusual. I would more characterize it as almost a perfect storm—it was a bunch of conditions and events coming together which made it possible.
>
> —A senior staff member

Using the adapted Kingdon model, the "perfect storm" can be disassembled and important actors and conditions can be identified. The following analysis shows that activity in the problem and policy streams led to the opening of a window of opportunity, which, combined with favorable activity in the political stream, allowed policy entrepreneurs to pursue their goals.

THE PROBLEM STREAM

According to Kingdon, how a problem is defined has implications for the likelihood of a problem getting placed on the government agenda and for the policy solution to which it becomes connected: "Conditions become defined as problems when we come to believe that we should do something about them" (Kingdon 1984).

One issue identified as a problem for NCLR was that the education debate was evolving, and NCLR's leadership felt that its policy priorities were keeping it out of the current debate. One board member recalled a need to develop an education agenda that responded to issues that were currently being debated—namely, accountability and standards and the school choice debate: "There wasn't a lot of focus in the philosophy behind what NCLR was doing in education—it seemed to be spotty attempts—education was becoming much more important and prevalent as an issue of concern in the Latino community, but we did not have anything that we could sink our teeth into at the organization level, except for the afterschool project that we were involved in.

Another active board member concurs: "At that time, charter schools was an issue that was in the air and NCLR had not taken a position; vouchers were also being discussed. So there were all kinds of proposals being considered that would affect the structure of education and we felt we needed to not hide from these changes but come out with a position."

In addition to board members and staff who felt that the absence of a strong education agenda was a problem, the Corporate Board of Advisors also expressed its concern. A board member recalls: "The Corporate Board of Advisors played a role in this too. There were some conversations there that they were concerned about the lack of educational advancement of Latinos. So some of those companies and foundations who were investing in education were turning to NCLR to frame a position."

The above discussion, however, does not explain why this problem would be elevated at this particular time. Interviews suggest, and will be detailed in the pages that follow, that a particular individual was essential to adding another element to the problem stream and raising the issue to a higher level. According to one staff member, one of the vice presidents was elemental in pushing the organization in a new direction:

> That was his whole pitch. He wanted to redesign our relationship with our affiliates to look more concretely at ways of sharing the resources. Because the resources were not getting there. There wasn't a community-development initiative. His whole thing was forming partnerships in a way that made a difference. He rolled out this whole thing—it was speech after speech across the country and a lot of that trickled into other aspects of the work. So

that when we started doing our strategic plan we considered how we are carrying out our work—looking at resources—how is that getting to the community?

As evidence of the organization's growing desire to directly provide resources to its affiliates, in 1998 NCLR established a community-development lending arm, the Raza Development Fund, Inc. (RDF). As detailed earlier in the organizational structure section, the fund works with affiliates to provide loans and technical assistance to local organizations.

For this vice president, the problem was that NCLR was not getting resources down to the affiliates, where the day-to-day work of improving outcomes was happening. This opinion resonated within the organization and the board, and influenced the decision-making process. According to a board member, "[T]here was increasingly a sense of how do we better serve our members and what are the issues that they are dealing with?" Within the problem stream, then, what we see is that changes in the education policy subsystem externally led to internal problem definition that was heavily influenced by individual leadership within the organization.

The Policy Stream

In the policy stream, multiple actors with varied opinions were influential in the goal-formation process. One staff member reflects the ambivalence about charter schools many felt on the policy side of the organization: "I've always felt from the beginning and I still feel skeptical about the ability of charter schools to impact large-scale reform—it's really hard for charter schools to look successful. Part of the reason we support charter schools is that we want to show that our kids are educable. And the only way we do that is to give others a sense of how to do that. That's a missing element in the charter school policy. I don't think any of that information is transferring over from charter schools [to the public school system]."

While individuals on the policy side were not sure what impact charter schools would have, those on the program side were enthusiastic supporters. One senior member of the staff with a strong connection to the grassroots and experience with charter schools identified the teachers unions as being the "largest problem" in reforming and improving education, a radical position for a member of NCLR's leadership to take. He also expressed frustration with organizations, NCLR included, that were not willing to consider new alternatives to respond to low educational attainment among Hispanics: "We need major, radical changes in the system, and some of them have to come from the outside. For NCLR, Aspira, and LULAC to think otherwise is to stick our heads in the sand. The system needs to be shaken up big-time."

While the policy team was busy conducting an analysis of charter schools and the programs division leadership was pushing for NCLR to support charters, the activity of the local groups was also visible in the policy stream. Raul Yzaguirre suggests that the time lag between Clinton's endorsement of charter schools in 1992 and NCLR's endorsement in 1999 was not based on the politics of charter schools: "There was no reason to take a position until our affiliates led us into that arena, and we essentially followed them." This is confirmed by an affiliate leader:

What caused NCLR to go in this direction [supporting charter schools] was already in the 1990s there were some people who were beating up on Yzaguirre and on NCLR for being on the margins—issuing all kinds of reports on the dropout rate and not going beyond that. There were in fact quite a few affiliates who were beating up on NCLR to do something. And then you have affiliates like ours who went out on their own without any NCLR support and started charter schools and then went back to NCLR and said, "Hey, look at what we're doing" and NCLR thought, "Hey, that ain't all that bad." And so I think it really went through a progression until NCLR finally realized, "Hey, maybe these affiliates are on to something here." And by that time some funders came around and quite frankly NCLR, I think, played a significant role in getting other affiliates onto the charter bandwagon.

One staff member recounts the situation faced by many of NCLR's affiliates that became interested in charter schools:

Charter schools weren't even on NCLR's map when I got hired. The main focus of the education work when I got there was supplemental programs for alternative schools or afterschool programs that were in our network. We had about twenty affiliates in our network that were alternative schools at the time. As we were doing that work, the charter laws were starting to get passed in different states, and these affiliates started calling us and asking us for information and for help learning about and applying for charter school status. So out of the alternative schools, their story was, "We've got a contract with the district, they pay us less than the public schools get, but we have to do more. They're giving us the kids they don't want; the dropouts, the kids with behavior problems, so we've got a population with more needs but we get less money. And depending on budget issues, we may not know if we're going to have a contract from one year to the next," so this charter thing looked pretty appealing to them, and they really pushed for our help.

One vice president also indicates that affiliates heavily influenced the activity of the Raza Development Fund and NCLR on charter schools:

> We initially thought that the affiliates—the partners that we were trying to serve—we thought there was going to be a big demand for housing funding. That's where our expertise was, and if you look at the community-development world, that's where the majority of capital was being expended. Well, to our surprise, the area that everyone wanted funding for was charter schools. So we are now the largest lender for charter schools in the country. . . . Charters weren't even on our radar screen at RDF, so we really just followed the affiliates, and I think that's why NCLR went in the direction they did too.

One staff member states it was the persistence of the affiliates that wanted to start charter schools that was critical to NCLR's actions:

> The affiliates didn't let up. A few of them said, "We're doing this with or without your help." So some of the bigger ones went ahead and applied. These were alternative schools that had been around for twenty years, and they had a lot of influence as affiliates and with the board. And they started bringing us statistics on what they were doing which were pretty compelling. And stories like that really started to change the perspectives of the VPs and the board. It made it clear that this wasn't about ideology; it was a practical way to serve our kids.

While a number of those interviewed emphasized the importance of members in bringing NCLR to the charter school debate, others suggest that while affiliate activity provided some of the momentum, additional factors influenced NCLR's decision-making. One said, "I don't think that it was that crystal clear. I think there was an evolution in our position; the affiliates were increasingly getting involved in education, there was a void nationally—NCLR was not really involved in education, and it was a question of where should we be at this particular point in time— it wasn't that clear—there was no idea of developing a huge program— that came after, and it evolved."

Another board member highlights the influence of affiliates, not as vocal proponents of charter schools but as providing examples of charter schools that were working for Hispanics: "I think that some of the affiliates had had very successful educational programs and we heard about them at the annual conferences and that provided folks the opportunity to see in action what the charter idea could do. So the direct experience of seeing how it might work was important."

While clearly there were affiliates that led the charge in support of charter schools, affiliates were not universally supportive of the movement. One affiliate leader points out that those affiliates with little exposure to operating education programs may have been more resistant:

> I remember sensing a very cool reception from many affiliates to the choice idea. I remember one of the early forums on choice at NCLR's annual conference there was some animosity regarding choice from many of the affiliates in the audience. When we were talking about choice in those days it meant that we were antiunion, that we were anti–public school. So those were some of the feelings that people had, not quite understanding what choice was. At the time, I would say that education as a real tool was not part of the affiliate network. Some of them may have been involved in alternative schools, but I don't think in the 1990s you had many affiliates at all who were heavy into providing education.

A board member confirms the hesitancy on the part of many affiliates to support charters and vouchers; "For the most part, I would say at that time, affiliates were leery about vouchers. And there was concern about charter schools. On the other hand, there was a recognition that some affiliates were already starting charter schools."

At NCLR's 2005 annual conference, informal conversation and observation of regional caucuses and workshop meetings revealed that charter schools were no longer a controversial issue among affiliates. Of the eight workshops held on the topic of education, two addressed charter schools. The first provided an overview of a particularly successful charter school in the Northeast, and the other explained how to receive a charter, get renewed, obtain foundation and philanthropic support, and finance school facilities. Two important points should be considered. First, in the time period between 1998 and 2005 affiliate leaders may have come to support charter schools after initially opposing the concept. Second, by 2005 the affiliate base included eighty charter schools, whose leaders obviously would be supportive. There may well have been more affiliates in 1998 that were uncomfortable with the charter school concept, but it appears as though the more vocal group was the affiliates that were opening charter schools and calling on NCLR for support.

This section shows that particular affiliates were aggressively pursuing the charter school option, while many other affiliates were hesitant to support charters. These two groups are likely divided by one characteristic: capacity. In an informal review of Hispanic serving charter schools in California, I found that community-based organizations that started charter schools in the California sample were at least twelve years old, and they were, as institutions, in a position to consider opening a charter school. They had the structure and access to resources, and running a charter school provided them with a reliable source of funding. Furthermore, as older and more established organizations, they possessed a stronger voice within NCLR. Therefore, their activity on charters had more impact on NCLR than the smaller, younger organizations that were opposed or undecided on the charter school question.

The policy stream within the organization was also heavily influenced by the policy alternatives available in the larger education-reform community. There was the sense from several individuals interviewed that Latino activists were frustrated with the lack of success of current policies and the limited alternatives available. According to an affiliate leader, "Those of us who supported choice said, OK, you don't like choice, but what are the other options out there? When you put it in that context, then people see that this is another option for us."

THE WINDOW OF OPPORTUNITY

Action in the problem and policy streams led to the opening of a window of opportunity: a task force on education appointed by the board of directors. As outlined in the problem stream section, in the late 1990s NCLR recognized the need to pursue priorities from a perspective other than its traditional "rights-focused" equity agenda. In a letter to a prospective funder, Yzaguirre recognized that issues such as vouchers and charter schools did not lend themselves to the traditional rights-focused approach. These new reform efforts, united under the banner of "excellence in education," convinced NCLR leadership that they needed to develop a policy agenda that would allow NCLR to be part of the current education debate. In order to determine their agenda, a task force was appointed. The task force would eventually endorse charter schools; according to a staff member, "Basically the task force endorsed the work on charter schools. The task force was important."

By late 1996, NCLR was in the process of obtaining funding for the education task force that would focus on the "excellence in education" movement. Funding requests proposed a task force examining the current literature to develop a framework for the task force's work, to commission reports, to meet with experts, and to oversee the development of a policy report and education agenda (December 6, 1996, letter to Carnegie Corporation of New York). By early 1997, six issues were identified that would be the focus of the task force's attention (February 14, 1997 letter to Carnegie Corporation of New York). These included standards-based reform, school choice (including vouchers and charters), classroom atmosphere, leadership in school administration, higher education, and early childhood programs. The task force was composed of academics, practitioners, affiliate representatives, and board members.

By the middle of its first year, the task force had narrowed the list to three issues that would be the focus of its attention: national testing and standards, school choice, and school leadership and administration. These issues were selected because members believed they required more immediate attention and had greater potential for impact than other education issues (progress report to the Carnegie Corporation of New York through June 1998). Hearings and meetings were held at the 1997 and 1998 annual conferences in order to obtain input from NCLR affiliates, practitioners, and researchers. The task force met in person approximately three times per year in order to review analysis completed by staff and to participate in roundtable discussions and panels with experts. Conference calls kept task members up-to-date between meetings. The long-term goal was the development of an education agenda for approval of the board. By October 1998, the school choice issue had been divided in two: charter schools and school vouchers. A memorandum directed to the board and prepared by staff on behalf of the task force on education suggested that the question of whether or not to support charter schools was more straightforward than the more controversial voucher issue (October 31, 1998, memorandum on school choice / charter schools / vouchers). Board members recollect considerable debate on the school choice issue, and one board member suggests that charter schools may have been the more palatable of the two options: "When you talk about charter schools, the next logical step would be vouchers, so charters may have been the compromise position. We kind of assumed that the families we served would not have the resources available to take advantage of vouchers." The discussions around charter schools, however, were also spirited; according to this board member: "There's always been the concern that charter schools would drain money from the public schools and what's going to be left for the other kids who can't get out of there. So I think that may have been the perspective of a lot of us in the debate on the board is that we're further strangling the ability of the public school system to serve our kids."

In the case of charter schools, the memorandum specified that a position in support of charters with certain provisos regarding quality, accountability, parental information, and opportunity to participate would not be inconsistent with its past positions. On vouchers, the memo authors were less positive. The memo refers to NCLR's traditional skepticism about market-based approaches to reform. Politically, while polls of

Hispanics and discussions with affiliates revealed that a majority support vouchers, the issue was supported by NCLR's traditional opponents and opposed by its traditional allies, including teachers unions and traditional civil rights groups. The recommendation of the memo was not to oppose vouchers, but to ensure that any voucher program be pilot-tested before embarking on a national program, and be equipped with appropriate safeguards to ensure adequate participation by Hispanics. At the April 1999 board meeting, the board adopted the task force language on charter schools verbatim, but strengthened its opposition to a voucher system unless the following issues were addressed:

- Latino parents have equal opportunity and access to exercise an informed choice to participate in the program;
- the program provides equal opportunity and access for participation of community-based schools; and
- the program includes rigorous documentation and evaluation systems to determine whether vouchers lead to improved achievement for participating disadvantaged students and/or positive public school reforms. (Memorandum to NCLR Task Force on Education, April 20, 1999)

Based on this decision, the first vice president of education was hired, and charter schools almost immediately became the fastest-moving issue in the organization.

THE POLICY ENTREPRENEUR

Policy entrepreneurs play a particularly important role in the extent to which policy alternatives are pursued and the amount of attention they receive from decision-makers—in this case, the board of directors of the organization. There is evidence that the presence of particular individuals played a decisive role in moving NCLR as an organization to a place where it was receptive to the charter school idea. According to a staff member,

It started when a new vice president came on board—maybe 1997. He came from one of the big community groups. He had ideas, and part of that was to think through a few things that I think were important. The first was to talk a lot more about impact—What impact were we having on the lives of people? Resources. The key was resources. If you really wanted to make a difference in lives of people, you had to have the money to do that. So finding a way of being able to deliver resources directly to people was the key, and I think that was a different way of looking at things.

As discussed in the problem stream section, this senior staff member, a vice president, in addition to being a supporter of charter schools, also vocally supported increased attention to community development at NCLR and the need for programs that funneled money to direct-service providers: "I was very supportive of charter schools and I always made that clear. . . . I also think the success we were having with the Partnership of Hope model—which dictated that you measure the impact on Hispanic families—really influenced how the board thought about charter schools." This vice president reveals that in addition to the community-development model that he was creating for the organization, he also had conversations with board members who were or became supporters of his approach to serving affiliates.

A strong individual in a leadership position, while not able to single-handedly redirect NCLR's resources, was clearly able to pose hard questions that the board of directors and the rest of the leadership clearly responded to. A staff member said, "What are we doing for these people was the real question he was asking, and nobody really had very good answers at the time." In addition, the presence of a more junior policy entrepreneur affected the scope of the project once the board had endorsed charters. According to one senior staff member, "She was key, because she had a vision of where we could go as an institution to support charter school development before the board took a position and before NCLR was ready to go there. So once we got the stamp of approval from the board, she was very aggressive. . . . So without her, we would be nowhere on charter school initiative. She was the visionary, but she was also the engine."

Interviews suggest that well before the board acted, this staff member was actively developing the expertise and connections necessary to launch a charter school campaign. A staff member commented, "So before the board approved of charters it was a little bit awkward, because it was kind of an unfunded mandate. I tried to learn whatever I could piggy-backing on other trips I had to make on the curriculum work that we were doing and even on my own time locally, volunteering with the charter schools that were getting started in DC."

Before board discussions began, this staff member pursued federal funding that would have allowed NCLR to enter into the charter school arena. This early effort was stopped by the vice presidents, as the staff member reported:

> Early in the days of the charter school movement it was conceptually aligned with vouchers and privatization and it was really something kind of taboo. So when we brought it to the VPs they were very hesitant to get engaged in charters. But the affiliates were adamant. They were going to do it and they needed our

help. So we decided to pursue a proposal from the Department of Education that was a charter school demonstration project. And we thought, this is the in. We'll apply for this and it will help us get up to speed on charter school law and so on. And we'll learn what we need to help these alternative schools convert. So it was a very particular niche; we weren't talking about vouchers or choice for ideological reasons, we were talking about underserved kids and the institutions that were serving them. We had to submit a preapplication, and we were approved and were invited to submit for the second round and that's when the VPs got nervous. I guess they thought we wouldn't make it to the second round, and we were told, "Don't do it, we don't have the capacity for this, this is too political," so we didn't get to apply for the second round. So that was a big blow.

Despite being discouraged to pursue this avenue of program development by the vice presidents of the organization, this staff member continued collecting data and learning about charter school law. By 1998, before board approval, the vice presidents decided that this staff member could move forward on charter schools.

So we finally got the green light from the VPs. In 1998 I then became sort of the point person on charter schools, going to conferences, visiting affiliates who had become charter schools, and visiting the alternative schools. Locally on my own time I was working with the charter schools here in DC to learn about the charter school law. In 1998 we started a pilot with Nueva Esperanza, which was one of our Philadelphia affiliates, to help them go through the charter school process. So I spent maybe six months helping them through the process. We did focus groups with teachers, parents, and kids to find out what they really wanted and design a school to complement what we heard. And after that we started the charter school development initiative.

This staff member suggests that the work she was involved in prior to board consideration informed the debate: "We had that work first before the board acted and that helped inform the process."

THE POLITICAL STREAM

The factors that are important in the political stream at the organizational level differ somewhat from Kingdon's model. In Kingdon's model, the actions of key national leaders and changes in the national mood are critical. At the organization level, the positions of an organization's traditional allies, one's membership, and key political leaders in the external political environment seem important to organizational leadership decision-making. While NCLR interviews indicate that ideology is not a serious constraint in its decision-making, one senior staff member, concerning the lag between the larger charter school movement and NCLR's entrance into the issue, recognized the politics of the movement, and said NCLR "wanted to make sure that we weren't captured by the Right on this issue." Another senior staff member also notes, "There's no question that our getting into charter schools appealed to a lot of people in the charter school movement, because the movement had been pegged as a right-wing movement, and they did not have good ties with the minority community, and when we got in, they were glad."

Although the charter school movement clearly came from the Right, it was eventually endorsed by key Democratic leaders, including former president Clinton. "The fact that Clinton triangulated the issue—that made it really easy all the way around," said a senior staff member. In addition to political factors outside of the organization, the ideological flexibility professed by NCLR leadership also plays an important role. A senior staff member said, "We were ideologically tolerant. I think we were one of the few groups that simultaneously were fully engaged with the traditional civil rights community and at the same time were separately seeking a Latino path. When issues like this came up, we weren't ideologically completely either left or right. It was a very natural thing. Whereas even for an Aspira, or a LULAC, or a MALDEF, that's much tougher. In case of MALDEF, they're firmly planted in the civil rights community. I think they are a more ideologically driven organization."

NCLR leadership was struggling as well to represent both a particular membership and the larger Hispanic constituency. One board member recalls:

> Certainly on the board of directors you had quite a few representatives of affiliates, and there was a heated debate on these issues. It was a long, difficult process on vouchers and also on charters. Ultimately what came out of the task force was a compromise between those groups—those that felt that we can't wait another generation for a comprehensive education reform, and those that felt we have to stay loyal to the system. And then we also had to take into account that both the African American community and the Latino community were in favor of charters and vouchers—the polls were clear. And so it seemed that the leadership was moving in one direction and the actual people were moving in another. And so a compromise was worked out where only under certain conditions would NCLR support charters and vouchers.

A senior staff member recalls that the board discussion on charter schools was contentious, reflecting the diverse perspectives held by board members: "I remember the board meeting on charter schools, and it was pretty hot. On that board there are some pretty Democratic members, and members connected to unions. The initial decision was to pass on charter schools, but that turned into a tacit support of charters by the end of the discussion."

Finally, NCLR was regarded by many in Washington as representing the Hispanic community, which made having an education agenda that reflected the current debates important. According to a board member, "NCLR had been involved in setting up the White House task force on education, and we had been part of various panels and hearings, so we were dabbling in education and folks were looking to us to provide some leadership and it was, OK, let's do it. So I think that was some of the pressure. . . . NCLR needed to be in the game, and the current education debate revolved around charters and standards."

Within the organization, the fact that the traditional division between program and policy had been overcome was also significant. One staff member recalls: "I was really the one pushing for it. I really carried the torch for charter schools. And after a while Charles [Kamasaki, senior policy vice president] really bought in. He saw the writing on the wall and saw that this was going to be the future for these Latino-serving schools. So once we got the policy shop behind it, it made it much easier, but it did originate on the program side."

The move to endorse charter schools is less clear in the political stream. Support for charters was far from universal; not all of NCLR's traditional allies had endorsed charter schools, and the opinions both within the leadership and among the membership were mixed. However, the support of key political leaders, such as President Clinton, polling data suggesting that Hispanics nationally supported charters, and the strong support from leadership within programs and among affiliates resulted in sufficient positive activity in the stream to allow for complete coupling.

SUMMARY

It seems clear that all five elements in the Kingdon model were essential to the birth and development of the charter school initiative. First, in the problem stream, a change in the national education debate and a perceived need to be part of that debate combined with a key individual within the organization who suggested that limited avenues for moving funding to affiliates was a problem. Second, in the policy stream, limited success with other policy alternatives frustrated actors both at the national and local levels, and there was a new policy alternative on the national scene that some

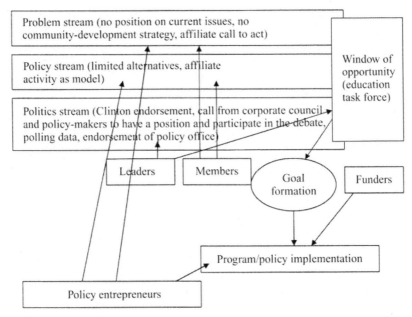

Figure 12. Goal formation at NCLR on charter schools

of the more vocal local groups were open to exploring. These currents combined to open a window of opportunity in the form of the education task force. Board members, concerned they were not influencing national education policy, formed a task force to determine NCLR's position on contemporary education issues, including charter schools. With the window of opportunity open, political stream activity also encouraged charter school endorsement. A receptive political climate at the national level and a flexible ideological position within the organization were important, as was the support of the policy division on this programmatic issue. Finally, policy entrepreneurs played multiple roles. A senior member of staff encouraged activity in the problem stream by pointing out the need to serve affiliates more directly. A more junior member of staff supported activity in the policy stream and developed the charter school program in advance of board action. This staff member also played an important role in the scope of the project that resulted.

As chapter 1 indicated, interest group theory suggests that organization leaders, members, or funders play decisive roles in organizational decision-making. My own analysis is that none of the three categories of actors on its own led the decision-making process. However, leaders and members clearly played essential roles. The leadership of the organization both called for NCLR to develop its education agenda and created the window of opportunity to make that happen. This was driven at least in part by a desire to more fully participate in national policy-making. The members—in this case, the affiliates—provided examples of charter schools that they had started without NCLR's help, and called on NCLR to assume a more active role in charter development.

Interviews suggest that NCLR did not develop its position on charter schools based on the potential for funding. According to one board member, "I don't recall that the task force was really feeling forced to move in one direction or another based on money being available. Although the movement was out there, the question, 'What position should we take?' more than 'What will we get out of it?' drove the work of the task force." In fact, the funders who were interested in funding charter schools were not traditional NCLR funders. This was another obstacle that programs staff needed to overcome. A staff member said:

> After the board approved it, it took a little while to get the funding approved, but we started working on a plan. . . . Our traditional education funders were not funding charter schools. And they were skeptical about us getting involved in the charter work. And so we did have a struggle in the beginning getting foundation support to do this kind of work. . . . We applied to a more conservative foundation, and the VPs had a meeting about it. And there were some pretty tense conversations about it. We were the only organization like NCLR that was buying into the charter schools.

That all of these stars needed to be aligned in order to have the outcome the organization did is evidenced by earlier efforts to get the charter program off the ground: "We didn't—we actually did a proposal in 1996 to get funding for charter school development but it was nixed by one of our VPs who didn't think it was important. It was one of those deals—people didn't know about charter schools much—there wasn't a clamor from the grassroots. . . ."

While many of the individuals involved recognized the important role affiliates played in the process, the majority of those interviewed agreed that there was not just one factor that moved NCLR to endorse charters. As a board member states, "It was a position that evolved over time with a lot of input from a variety of sources."

CONCLUSION

National Council of La Raza has emerged as an organization that can be successful on multiple levels. At the national policy-making level, NCLR is recognized as a powerful advocate for Hispanic interests. Through the charter school initiative, NCLR has also shown that it can overcome expected ideological positions and marshal its resources in response to the needs and desires of local Hispanic organizations. The charter school experience reveals a great deal about NCLR and how it functions. Several findings stand out.

The presence of a policy entrepreneur within the organization significantly impacts the scope, if not the direction, of the organization's agenda. While charter schools is probably the most dramatic example of this, discussions with NCLR staff reveal a willingness among NCLR leadership to give staff the freedom to pursue their own interests. Certainly in the case of charter schools, staff aggressively pursued funding and an ambitious program within the organization. This freedom led to a shift in the pillars, making the program pillar significantly larger, but based on only one program. The result was a very strong charter school program, which was extremely valuable to those affiliates which were well established and had the capacity to use NCLR's assistance to develop a charter school. Some staff, however, recognize that most of NCLR's affiliates do not have the capacity to take advantage of that opportunity. One senior staff member commented:

> Right now, the real question for NCLR is "Who are our affiliates and how do we grow our affiliate base?" Because from the perspective of RDF, if the affiliate base doesn't grow over the next two years, we will have saturated our market. In the charter school industry, we just negotiated a deal that will put together a $50 million fund just for charter schools. And looking at the charters in our affiliate base right now, I couldn't spend it all. So we either grow the affiliates or we run into problems with investors, who will take their money somewhere else.

Given the considerable fund-raising ability of NCLR, the organization's leadership must do more to hold entrepreneurs in check and be a conduit for appropriate funding and technical assistance to those younger and less-established organizations.

My case study of NCLR also reveals a division between policy and programs that was overcome in the case of charter schools. In this instance, charter schools were a policy alternative that was not viewed favorably by the policy division but gained the support of key players on the program side, who then influenced the policy side. This appears to be an unusual case for the organization in that the program side influenced the policy side, which led to a change in the organization's policy position on charter schools.

More broadly, the view expressed earlier that there is a division between DC-based groups and those outside of Washington could also be applied to the program and policy divisions within NCLR. Using the continuum offered earlier, it may be that while the policy division is further along the continuum in the direction of decision-making, those on the program side (and therefore closer to the grassroots) are closer to the "speak truth to power" end.

The case study reveals a complex decision-making process within a sophisticated national-level organization, heavily influenced by its desire to be influential at the national policy-making level but also increasingly looking to its local affiliates as policy innovators. The next section explores the response to charter schools by LULAC, a considerably different organization, with a much stronger connection to the grassroots that results in a very different goal-formation process.

LULAC's Response to Charter Schools

To date, LULAC has not taken an official position on charter schools, but has been outspoken in its opposition to vouchers. In many of the interviews, when asked to discuss LULAC's position on charter schools, participants responded by describing the organization's position on vouchers. An example of this is one former president's description of charters, which conflates charters and vouchers: "If I want my child to go to this charter school and take that money from this inner city school and take it with that child to that other school—it could be a private school, maybe religious-based—look, if someone wants to take their child to a private school, then you should pay for that with your own money. The public schools are there to serve everybody. . . ."

While further discussion clarified that some participants did understand the difference between charters and vouchers, even then their position was that charters and vouchers were more alike than different. As one former president says, "We don't support charter schools, we don't support vouchers in any way. It's part of our agenda for the organization. We feel that vouchers in any way, and charters is included in that, take away from the public system and eventually they will hurt more people than they will help. We support public schools, and that's why we don't support any kind of effort to take anything away from the system. . . . We feel charter schools are just an alternative under vouchers."

The individuals interviewed were clear that the organization was opposed to vouchers. Moreover, while some were uncertain about the organization's official position on charters, all made the connection between vouchers and charters. This position appears to be an instinctive response, rather than one based on research or analysis of charter schools. This is evident in comments by another former president: "LULAC has always opposed vouchers for the simple reason that the public school system is the one that is going to educate our children. On charter schools, I don't know whether we have taken a position, but I believe they have to be viewed with some reservation, because some charters really segregate. In areas where there are high minority populations, charter schools are created in order to serve only a particular population. I would say the general consensus at LULAC is that charters are not a good thing for the public education system."

While this former president suggests charters are organized to serve the nonminority population, one vice president believes charters are designed to segregate minority students: "Historically, our position has been that we oppose charter schools, primarily because we believe our children have a right to a free public education. And charter schools are offering a different alternative and it's wrong, because we have found, if you look at charter schools, they end up becoming a separate entity and students of color are put there and it's another form of segregation."

Though, in fact, the evidence is mixed, a former president suggests that research shows charter schools are not academically successful. This same leader is also concerned that charter schools will not provide the resources public schools can, such as free lunch. (In fact, charter schools are funded to provide free lunches to all students who qualify.) And despite the existence of a considerable number of schools created specifically to serve a particular cultural group, this leader suggests that charter schools may not be culturally sensitive: "Most schools—there is no charter school that is opened and maintained by their own money. And all the research shows that they're not doing any better than the public schools, they're doing worse. And they don't have the long history of dealing with Hispanic children that have limited English proficiency and all the problems that our kids come to school with. The public schools feed a lot of kids through the free lunch program. That's not going to happen at the charter school."

One member who has held statewide office within LULAC has a very different perspective on charter schools:

> High schools right now are really stuck in the old ways of doing business. In spite of the many reform efforts, many school districts continue to function in the same way they always have. These schools have failed to effectively change with the changing needs of Hispanic communities. So I support charter schools because charters may do it differently, smaller, and better, and hopefully that will improve the public school system. That is a change in my position from five years ago, but that's because I have seen very little change in the public education system, and

> I think having a competitive alternative may be what we need right now. Now that's not LULAC's position. I've talked to [the LULAC president] about LULAC's position on charter schools, and he did think that it was an issue we may have to consider.

One staff member identifies the sources of resistance to charter schools within LULAC: "There are a lot of teachers in LULAC, and so anything that threatens the public school system is a serious problem. And many LULAC members see charter schools as the beginning of a move toward a voucher system. Especially in Texas you see a lot of that, and Texas members have a lot of influence."

Between 1998 and 2000, the LULAC national assembly passed five resolutions affirming their opposition to vouchers. None of the five resolutions made a direct reference to charter schools, but implied that LULAC would oppose any effort that would weaken the traditional public school system.

Goal Formation and Charter Schools

LULAC formed a national education task force in 2002 similar to the NCLR task force on education that provided the window of opportunity for NCLR's charter schools program. The interviews conducted for this book provided a variety of interpretations of the history, genesis, and role of the task force. It is clear that the task force was formed in order to establish an education agenda and identify issues that would be the focus of its advocacy efforts. On other questions, such as when it was started, who was involved, and whether it was still active, there were a number of different opinions, as well as a lack of knowledge, by members of the current board of directors.

Kingdon's model highlights several patterns in LULAC's decision-making. The process that occurred around education decision-making at LULAC in the 2002/2003 time period illuminates the influence of particular members and the effect on decision-making of the highly politicized nature of the organization.

The Problem Stream

In the problem stream, the overwhelming response from interview participants was that low educational attainment in the Hispanic community was a serious problem, both for Hispanics and for the country. One former president's comments echo those from many of those interviewed: "There are a multitude of issues that impact the Latino community in education, and one of the most noted problems that needs to be resolved is that the schools where Latinos are enrolled are not well funded to serve their special needs. And then there are so many Latinos who work, but because their salaries are low, they can't support their families, and so the older children in the family drop out of school to work so that they can contribute."

Specifically, participants tended to emphasize the dropout problem and the need to find solutions. Apart from the model offered by the LULAC National Educational Service Centers, interviewees had difficulty connecting the dropout problem to policy alternatives being considered at the national level. Unlike at NCLR, interviews did not suggest that LULAC leadership thought it was a problem for the organization that they were not participating in the education policy debate at the national level.

THE POLICY STREAM

In the policy stream, there are a number of established education programs and policy positions accepted across the organization. Locally, many of the councils raise funds for a scholarship program, and the LULAC National Educational Service Centers, as described earlier, provides a range of educational services to middle school and high school youth.

At the national assembly, recent education issues voted on were not controversial and supported positions already present in the legislative platform of the organization. In 2002, the three education resolutions at the national convention included a call for universal prekindergarten education, support for the Reading Recovery program, and support for a case submitted to the Office of Civil Rights regarding discriminatory practices at a school in Arizona. In 2003, the national assembly passed a resolution to launch an information campaign for LULAC's scholarship program and a resolution in support of bilingual education.

Interviews and analysis of resolution votes and the legislative platform suggest that charter schools were clearly not an acceptable policy alternative for LULAC members. One staff member says this of his efforts at raising the issue of charter schools for consideration:

> We haven't endorsed them but we haven't opposed them either. One time I tried to put into the platform that we would support charter schools as a way of providing some choice in the public school system, but it got voted down saying that they don't support charter schools. They didn't make me put in language that they oppose charter schools but they wouldn't support them. It was a plank that I wanted to add to the legislative platform, but that got voted down. I think that was in 2001. A number of the

people who were opposed were educators, and they said that still took money from public schools and also that the quality of the charter schools was hit or miss.

One alternative in the policy stream did attract more attention at the national level and led to a flurry of education policy activity. This alternative was the education summit model developed by a LULAC member in Illinois. The Illinois state director describes the genesis of the project: "The education commission was started because the state of Illinois brought this idea to the national board of directors. We were a pilot program. So they established the education commission that now seeks funding for the project in Illinois and other states."

Though interview responses varied widely on the timing of events, there were three entities that were created around this time; the first was the summit model to address the dropout problem. Second, there was a task force on education, apparently organized as a result of the creation of the summit model. Third, a commission was created, either before or after the task force. One staff member close to the events suggests that the first summit in Illinois led to the appointment of a commission; that led to the appointment of a task force, which will be identified as the window of opportunity: "The whole thing started with the Illinois summit, which laid the foundation for the task force and the commission. The task force was very ad hoc; it was led by the grassroots, particularly from the state of Illinois. The task force evolved from the commission."

Within LULAC, the role of commissions varies, but they are largely charged with developing a policy alternative and pursuing funding so that the model or program can be replicated in different parts of the country. A senior staff member said, "The committees identify programs or funding ideas, and once that happens a commission is formed. A commission is not formed unless it gets funding and the board also makes sure that the commission is controlled by LULAC and doesn't get away from their control, like sometimes happens to LULAC."

Those interviewed had a general understanding of the role and purpose of the education commission, an understanding reflected in a former president's description of the program: "The commission was a permanent commission—we have people who have been successful in their school districts. So we're putting together a kind of presentation that we're taking across the country and bringing local people in to see what's being done in other parts of the country and to see what maybe they can do in their district to improve the Latino dropout rate." Opinion is mixed, however, with regard to the success of the national commission. Commissions appear to get appointed and often drift, depending on who is leading them and whether their activities are receiving funding. One board member's comments on the education commission reflect a sentiment shared by a number of those interviewed:

> LULAC's Education Commission is supposed to go to the different regions and inform the school authorities about the problems we have with the dropout rate. I'm not too familiar with the work of the commission. I know that the last two meetings of the board they haven't provided a report. I think it's been a couple of years now that they haven't reported. I know they're supposed to meet and provide programs. I don't think that's been happening. As a matter of fact, I submitted a proposal to the national board, because I wanted an education summit in [my state] and we're working on trying to get that together. But I haven't heard back from them.

Others interviewed concur that their impact has been limited, and that education policy advocacy and programming continues to be driven by the local councils. As a board member remarks, "The national education commission has put on some events related to dropout prevention in the state of Texas. The national education commission is not really a . . . it's put on a couple of things that I know of—conferences—in Texas. But in terms of the policy, that's generally done at the grassroots level."

Like this board member, another board member does not consider the commission to be leading education policy within the organization: "The president has done a good job on forming commissions—there are lots of commissions now. The commission on education has held some educational summits where they bring educators in and get input on the programs that are working for dropouts. My concern is that the dropout problem is a big one, and we can have summits, but we need to come up with a plan of action. That's the thing that I see is missing sometimes."

Some members suggest that the availability of funding determines the attention a commission receives A board member says: "At this last board meeting, I expected a report from the education commission, but they weren't on the agenda—only the housing commission was on the agenda. Right now that's the commission that's a big deal, because they're getting funding. That's really when you pay attention to a commission: when they're getting funding."

A staff member confirms the importance of funding for commission survival: "There was supposed to be a series of summits; the next one was supposed to be in California, but I couldn't get the funding together for it. That's part of the challenge. There are great ideas, but we have to raise the money to do these things. And that's been hard."

A board member close to advocates of the summit model opined that, in addition to developing a replicable model, the education commission has been successful because it does not have high funding requirements. Her comments are particularly interesting, because they contrast with those of others who felt the commission on education had stalled. She said,

> I think the education summit has been so successful because the dropout problem is a national problem and the other councils can use this model. The models we send to the national office are things that can be copied anywhere in the country. That is why the summit has become so popular. . . . The first summit, we didn't ask for national funding from LULAC. After that, we asked for some funding from the national office and we raised some of the money. We tried to keep the spending very low so that we could do it. When we first asked for money for the first summit, we were denied. But the later summits were funded— they would give us maybe $2000, and we would raise a matching amount. We don't spend much, which makes it easier for the national office to give us the money.

Interviews suggest that, apart from the education commission summits, the development of policy alternatives at the national level within LULAC is limited. Local councils have limited financial resources, may not have sufficient expertise to develop replicable programs, and face political obstacles within the organization. One interviewee, a state-level leader, also suggests that the national staff, which perhaps could be developing program ideas, are too overwhelmed with responding to issues as they arise to dedicate time to proactive program development: "NCLR has been very active in pursuing the charter school concept, and I commend them for it. I think they've worked very hard to develop alternatives. LULAC is more grassroots, and they become more active in their own arena and not at the national level. And also our national staff doesn't really look at programs, they really just are reacting to policy issues."

Within the policy stream, then, the only active education policy alternative was the summit model created by the education commission. It seems clear that the ability of commissions to succeed is based directly on their ability to garner funds from outside of the organization. The following sections will help to explain why the education commission's work was limited to holding summits.

THE POLICY ENTREPRENEUR

Using the Kingdon model and analyzing the education activity at LULAC in the period around 2000, there was clearly an entrepreneur who was able to bring his policy alternative to life at the national level. According to a former president, "The reason why the education commission has gone in the direction it has is the work of Manny Isquierdo, who was a school principal at the time. And he is kind of the mover behind what the commission is doing."

A state director suggests that the commission was driven by the success of the summit in Cicero, which Isquierdo developed: "Before you establish a commission, you have to have a pilot program. And that was the educational summit. The idea came from Dr. Manuel Isquierdo. He volunteered for the education committee when I was the state director of Illinois. So he brought the principals, counselors, students, and LULAC members together."

Interviews suggest that commissions, while influenced by the funding available, as mentioned earlier, are also heavily swayed by the strength of the leadership within the commission and the connection between the commission leadership and the organizational leadership. In this case, the commission originally had the strong support of organizational leadership. A board member says, "That's another thing that's unique—the commissions kind of evolve—like a lot of what happens in LULAC, a lot of what the commissions do is based on what a few key leaders within LULAC want to do on something."

Some interview participants also reported that in the event commission leadership was to lose favor with organizational leadership as a result of political disagreements, commissions may cease to be funded. While it is unclear whether this is what happened in the case of the education commission, it is clear that the volunteer nature of the organization, combined with limited resources, provides opportunities for individuals to promote their own agendas through the development of commissions and/or task forces.

THE WINDOW OF OPPORTUNITY

In 2002 a task force was formed to address education policy issues. One former president explains why the task force got started: "It's always been a great concern of ours—it's in our pledge, in our motto, that we pursue the educational advancement of Latinos in this country. And we felt we had to pay attention to different ways that we could bring this issue into focus." More concretely, a staff member describes as follows the chain of events that led to the creation of the commission and the task force:

I contacted different experts within LULAC on education after the presentation on the summit at a board meeting. I thought the presentation was great, and so I said we need to get this down on paper. They gave me outlines. But I said, "You guys really need a group to do this. It shouldn't come from me, it should come from you." But I facilitated that. So I took information from all the people on the task force, who are LULAC volunteers, LNESC [LULAC National Educational Service Centers] staff, and some outside people. And all of these people gave me text, and I cobbled this thing together, based on the perspectives of all these different people, practitioners and policy analysts.

The use of the term "ad hoc" seems appropriate here; the task force was fashioned from whatever resources (i.e., members) were readily available. They produced a paper and then seem to have disbanded. In addition, like all other aspects of LULAC, it appears as though political dynamics affect the organization and dissolution of task forces, and the education task force in particular. One staff member hinted at this when asked to explain why committees and task forces can stall: "Power shifts within the organization, and power relationships shift. So you have the challenges of being volunteer-based, a decentralized system, and shifts in power." In her comments she also reveals a disconnect between member activities and staff: "There was a task force; I don't know if it has continued. The membership changes all the time . . ."

The task force was started in February 2002. By June 2002, an education agenda was released that outlined the organization's major concerns and priorities in the education arena. The agenda that resulted from task force deliberations offers twelve recommendations for education reform (Lemus 2002). It requests increased funding for community-based organizations, parental involvement programs, school infrastructure, and bilingual education. The agenda also recommends that the needs of undocumented and migrant children be addressed, that standards of teaching and counseling be improved, and that elected officials and government agencies be held accountable. The agenda does not make recommendations on charter schools or high-stakes testing, arguably two of the most controversial and high-profile education issues facing policy-makers.

A former state director emphasizes the critical role in policy decision-making played by the task forces: "The task force recommends to the president programs or projects or support of policies. That's why we need to have a task force. I don't know why we don't have a task force right now. Maybe it's just that now there is an education committee but not a task force. . . ."

The task force on education does not seem to fit the model as understood by this interviewee. There does not appear to have been a thorough fact-finding process or any consideration of issues that members had not already endorsed. As several interviews suggested it seems as though the volunteer nature of the work, funding problems, and political dynamics combined to limit the work of the task force to the publication of an agenda that reiterated the policy alternatives LULAC was already on record as supporting.

THE POLITICAL STREAM

Within such a politically driven organization, it is not surprising that the political stream is very influential. Regarding vouchers and charters, individuals in leadership who choose to be supportive of school choice pay a heavy political price. Several interviewees recalled the difficulties faced by one leader in LULAC who suggested the organization consider the charter-schools policy alternative. A staff member said, for instance: "She supported vouchers and the members got furious because she said some things favorable towards vouchers and they were outraged. It's not a tepid position that we have." And a past president commented: "Now on vouchers, the position is very clear. In fact . . . they filed impeachment charges because she started advocating vouchers . . . they were going to kick her out of the organization. I was the president at the time, and I didn't want to kick her out because she'd been with the organization for twenty-five years. So I talked to the folks . . . and we worked out a censure, but that's how strongly members feel about the vouchers issue."

The influence of members is clear in this case. Leadership was aware that a position in support of vouchers would alienate some significant part of the organization's voters. The member in question appears to be intentionally vague in her response to a question on vouchers: "I actually don't know much about the vouchers. . . . I know that LULAC has national resolution against vouchers. The concern is that money would be taken from the public school system and given to the private system."

SUMMARY

Kindgon's model reveals an organization with a decision-making process that is dominated by the force of the political stream. The priority of the problem stream is the concern that Hispanics continue to have unacceptably high dropout rates. This feeds into the activity in the policy stream, where a summit is developed as a model for addressing the dropout problem. An education commission is formed to formalize the summit model.

As a result of this new policy alternative in the policy stream, a window of opportunity is opened in the form of an education task force. On the surface, it appeared as though LULAC's task force was an opportunity to explore all of the current education policy alternatives being debated at the national level and to revise LULAC's education agenda. In fact, this task force was simply an opportunity to collect already established opinions from grassroots leadership and combine them in a document that could be used at the national level. As illustrated in figure 13, the window of opportunity was, as a result, not actually open. This was because the political stream did not support a full exploration of policy alternatives. In the case of charter schools, it was noted earlier that one leader attempted to bring the choice issue to the table, but her efforts were quickly and forcefully stopped by the Texas membership. Charter schools have been a subject that members have been unwilling to consider. Members and leaders have strongly denounced vouchers and, by extension, charters. The political strength of the organization is at the grassroots level, which limits the ability of Washington paid staff to explore policy alternatives that may depart from traditional LULAC positions. As a result of the action in the political stream, what we see is a window of opportunity that is not a real opening, as it does not provide for the exploration of new policy alternatives.

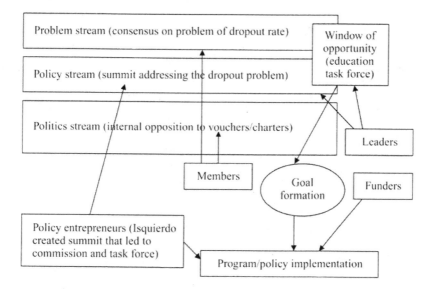

Figure 13. Goal formation at LULAC on education policy

Conclusion

LULAC is an organization with extremely strong connections to the grass-roots. Looking at the three potential sources of influence in their decision-making—leaders, funders, and members—we see that leaders are heavily influenced by members, while funders appear to play no role at all.

Unlike the view expressed by Marquez (2003b) that corporate sponsorship weakened LULAC's connection to its membership, my research finds that the concerns of membership prevail throughout the organization. Earlier I suggested that Marquez's methodology was not sufficient to conclude that LULAC is ruled by funding needs and funder preferences. In his study Marquez compares the amount of money the organizations in the study receive from foundation sources to income from membership dues. From this he suggests that the organizations rely on, and as a result are influenced by, a small number of funding sources and wealthy individuals, and are disconnected from a membership base. My own study concludes that while members may not have the final say on each policy position LULAC takes and though board leadership may have some ability to adopt positions not fully supported by the membership, ultimately members have a very strong voice that, once heard, is very hard, if not impossible, to ignore. School choice is an excellent example of this; once the membership decides through the resolutions process that they oppose a policy alternative, the organization's position is steadfast, regardless of changes in the alternatives available. As for organizational leadership, leaders are loath to offend their membership, who appear to be only too happy to use their voting power to make sure their leadership is representing them. While most interview respondents acknowledged that charter schools were different from a voucher system, the memory of one leader's near removal from LULAC because of her support of school choice may be enough for leadership to leave the choice issue alone. Finally, funders play no apparent role in LULAC's decision-making. While LULAC may pursue a program idea if a particular funder is willing to sponsor it, national leadership and, particularly, paid staff do not have the ability to change their policy positions to suit the desires of funders.

6

Goal Formation on Immigration Reform

A Brief History of Immigration Reform

Before the end of the nineteenth century, the United States was unconcerned with restricting immigrant flows, and left immigration rule-making to the states. By the end of the nineteenth century, however, the public mood shifted, and the federal government took a more active interest in controlling flows of immigrants. The first group to be targeted was the Chinese, who as a result of prejudice were essentially banned entry to the United States. By the time the National Origins Act of 1924 was passed, economic tensions combined with racial and religious intolerance to reduce immigration to 150,000 places for Europeans, with a focus on northern and western Europe. By the 1940s, legal immigration was tightly controlled, and Mexican and Chinese immigrants were rare. This would slowly change in the 1940s and 1950s, leading to a major liberalization of immigration law in the 1960s.

In 1943, Congress repealed the Chinese Exclusion Act, and through a number of different acts allowed refugees from war-torn countries to immigrate. These smaller moves toward liberalization culminated in the Hart-Cellar Immigration Act of 1965. The act called for the admission of immigrants based on their professional skills, occupation, and relationship to families in the United States. Rather than a national origins quota, the bill imposed a preference system, with seven ranked categories: children of U.S. citizens, immediate family members of permanent resident aliens, highly skilled workers, married sons and daughters and siblings of U.S. citizens, skilled and unskilled workers deemed to be in short supply, and refugees.

An annual limitation of 170,000 visas was established for immigrants from Eastern Hemisphere countries, with no more than 20,000 per country. By 1968, the annual limitation from the Western Hemisphere was set at 120,000 immigrants, with visas available on a first-come, first-served basis. These numbers do not accurately reflect total immigration, as admissions of refugees from Cuba, Vietnam, Laos, and Cambodia were in the hundreds of thousands. Nevertheless, the act revolutionized the criteria for immigration to the United States, and ushered in a new era of immigration law in this country.

In the latter half of the twentieth century, immigration reform policies became more prominent on the national agenda, and immigrant advocates increasingly played a role in crafting legislation. The system established with the Hart-Cellar law has been repeatedly tested and reshaped over the past several decades; three major reforms were the Immigration Reform and Control Act of 1986, the Immigration Act of 1990, and the Illegal Immigration Reform and Immigration Responsibility Act of 1996. This chapter focuses on the immigration law passed in 1986 and then assesses the positions of NCLR and LULAC in the current immigration-reform debate.

The Immigration Reform and Control Act of 1986

In the decade following enactment of the 1965 law, immigration numbers soared. In addition to a rise in legal immigration, a combination of a worsening Mexican economy and an ending of the Bracero program in 1964 (which had allowed employers to hire Mexicans on a temporary basis) led to a rise in undocumented immigration. The demand for low-wage agricultural workers only grew in the 1970s, which led to a significant increase in the number of Mexicans crossing the border illegally. Some unscrupulous employers used their workers' undocumented status to abuse workers and threaten deportation if they complained. By the 1970s, undocumented immigration became the focus of public debate, and there was a growing tide of support for employer sanctions that punished employers who hired undocumented immigrants. The Select Commission on Immigration and Refugee Policy was created in 1978 as a response to dramatic increases in immigration and was given two years to develop an immigration remedy. A report released by the commission in early 1981 suggested that employers be sanctioned for knowingly hiring illegal aliens. It also recommended a onetime amnesty that would permit aliens in the United States before January 1, 1980 to become legal immigrants—at the time an estimated 4 to 6 million persons were living in the United States illegally. It did not recommend a large-scale temporary-worker program. Its proposals were controversial, and it would be several years before legislation would be passed addressing immigration reform.

The Immigration Reform and Control Act of 1986 was the first attempt to address the problem of undocumented immigration. The main element of this bill was to impose sanctions on employers who hired undocumented immigrants. The bill also created an amnesty program, which provided a path to citizenship for 2.7 million undocumented immigrants, including 2 million Mexicans. The act also substantially increased funding for the border patrol. Hispanic and immigrant rights groups played an important role in the debate and passage of this bill, and many argue it was NCLR's leadership that finally made passage possible.

The Hispanic groups did not share the same position on employer sanctions, and their positions changed dramatically in the years leading up to the 1986 law. Among the groups that initially supported employer sanctions legislation was LULAC. LULAC's original mission, as previously mentioned, supported only legal immigrants. LULAC endorsed Operation Wetback, a 1954 federal campaign that aggressively deported Mexicans back to Mexico, and in many cases accidentally entangled U.S. citizens and legal immigrants in its net. By the 1970s, new leadership and the civil rights era moved LULAC in a different direction, one that emphasized immigrant rights and eventually denounced employer sanctions. From the start, MALDEF opposed employer sanctions on the basis of civil rights. Its concern, which would later be borne out, was that Hispanics regardless of citizenship status would be discriminated against as employers struggled to enforce immigration law. Like MALDEF, NCLR had from the outset opposed employer sanctions; its internal debate focused on how much of its political capital should be spent on the issue, with paid leadership pushing to make it a top priority and board members harboring mixed opinions. By the 1980s, the three Hispanic groups had come to strongly and publicly oppose employer sanctions, arguing that this measure would only lead to discrimination against legal immigrants and citizens of Hispanic origin. The issue of temporary workers also seems to have been universally opposed by these groups on the grounds that a temporary-worker system provided employers with a flexible employee base but offered the workers no protection against labor law violations; the groups organized the National Hispanic Task Force on Immigration Policy, which opposed all temporary-worker programs.

Outside of the Hispanic community, however, there was a sense in the 1980s that immigration was out of control, and employer sanctions were seen as a viable solution. The Select Commission on Immigration and Refugee Policy recommendations were drafted into legislation that was opposed by NCLR, LULAC, MALDEF, and others, including leadership in the broader civil rights community and in the business community, who were also opposed to employer sanctions on the grounds that employers should not bear responsibility for enforcing immigration law. Initial attempts at passage met with failure, largely due to this varied opposition.

Eventually, however, influential elements within the opposition to the bill began to peel away. A senior staff member at NCLR recalls:

> So it wasn't quite a coalition in the sense that people didn't sit down at a table and say, "Here's the target that we're going to meet," but there were groups working in parallel to each other that could collectively get enough votes to keep it from moving forward, really by the skin of their teeth. If it takes a Speaker blocking a conference report—which is what happened the first time—we were just barely beating it. What ended up happening was that the growers decided that the writing was on the wall and that they weren't going to be able to stop it. And so rather than continuing to put all of their energy in opposing it, they started to work out a deal on an agricultural workers legalization program. They figured that if they were going to get hammered by employer sanctions, they should make sure they could get a program out of it. And when that started to happen, we also saw the writing on the wall.

LeMay's analysis of the lobbying leading up to passage of the immigration act of 1986 suggests that Hispanic groups as a whole decided that it was necessary to compromise (LeMay 1994). While he identifies NCLR's Charles Kamasaki as a key player at the bargaining table with committee staff, the assumption is that the other groups also recognized that the time had come to broker a deal. Other authors (and I myself) distinguish between the groups and identify a divergence of opinion on the decision to compromise. As found by Sierra (1991) and confirmed in interviews for the present study, after years of working in coalition to obstruct passage of an immigration reform bill whose major element was employer sanctions, NCLR decided that some form of immigration bill was inevitable and that it was time to negotiate. MALDEF maintained its strong opposition to any bill that involved employer sanctions or a guest-worker program, and LULAC also continued to be opposed, though with less intensity than MALDEF due to internal organizational changes. It was at this time that a key policy entrepreneur left the debate, influencing more than just LULAC's role. His absence was likely felt across the Hispanic advocacy community. Sierra (1991) notes the important role played by Arnoldo Torres at LULAC in garnering media attention and lobbying Congress. An aggressive and forceful lobbyist, his resignation in 1985 resulted in a lower-profile role for LULAC in the immigration debate in subsequent years. As a result of diverging positions, collaboration between the groups decreased significantly.

The Current Immigration-Reform Debate

With the Democratic victories in the 2006 midterm elections, advocates for immigration reform on both sides of the issue began to mobilize for a legislative debate. The main elements were not radically different from earlier debates around the 1990 and 1996 laws; NCLR and others argued that the laws have failed both as a result of weaknesses in execution of employer sanctions and because of economic realities. A senior staff at NCLR summarizes the situation as follows:

> Sanctions failed, in part, because they weren't really structured to work well. It really isn't enforceable without some kind of national document policy, which the country wasn't, and arguably still isn't, ready for. But the other reason is that there is a market for this labor. So the flow of undocumented immigrants still continued at the same pace, a pace which increased over time, but increased steadily. There was no kind of major wave that happened. The estimated rate of undocumented migration of people who would come and stay was about two hundred and fifty [thousand] to three hundred thousand in the 1980s. And it's between three hundred fifty [thousand] to four hundred thousand now. So there was kind of a steady increase. And there are periodic surges and declines. When the peso got devalued, there was a surge, for example. But by and large, it's a continuous pace. So that was really the thing IRCA [the Immigration Reform and Control Act of 1986] didn't do—was acknowledge that there was a need for that labor and that the market for that labor was going to be strong enough to continue.

This staff member recognizes that there have been a number of attempts to enforce immigration law over the last two decades, but none have staunched the flow:

> There was another reform in '96, which was all about making it harder for people to enter, making it harder for people once they got here. Even in the debate leading up to that in the Clinton administration it really was in enforcement—that was when Ricky Jervais at the El Paso border implemented what they called "Operation Hold the Line." And they invested so heavily in the San Diego sector that they succeeded in controlling the flow so that people went around, and that's how we got the death toll. So there was a huge investment in enforcement, which has changed

the flow to the extent that it has changed where it happens and it has added to the death toll—people who die crossing the desert. Which is huge, more every year. Which is now, you know, the staple of the way immigration happens now.

Some advocates support reduced numbers of allowed immigrants and stronger border enforcement. Others are focused on easing the logjam in the citizenship application process, developing a solution for qualified unauthorized workers already in the country, and creating pathways to earn eventual permanent residence. With regard to illegal immigration, the debate centers on how to resolve the status of the estimated eleven million undocumented immigrants already in the United States. While few suggest wholesale expulsion, there are varied approaches to the problem, including demands for a reliable employment-verification system that is combined with new temporary and permanent visas to meet the needs of employers.

NCLR has not backed away from its conditional acceptance of employer sanctions, despite the fact that the existing sanctions program is a failure. NCLR and others continue to work to develop a proposal on a national identification card that would be palatable to all sides of the debate. Says a staff member at NCLR:

> So our positions both on employer sanctions and the temporary worker program have evolved over that time. . . . And we are all showing IDs everywhere we go anyway, so let's try to create a system that is more likely to give employers the confidence that they are actually hiring the people they should be hiring. And let's try to design it in a way so we minimize the potential dis- crimination against workers. So there's a working group, with- out a name, but working together informally that includes us, the ACLU, the Chamber of Commerce, and a bunch of other actors, that has essentially devised a compromise agreement on how sanctions should work.

NCLR came to their approach to immigration reform and their ac- ceptance of some form of national ID after considering the tenor of the immigration debate, particularly post-9/11. An NCLR staff member says,

> Last year, the National Conference of State Legislatures counted about five hundred anti-immigrant pieces of state legislation that were introduced all over the country. We are never going to win those battles one at a time. The only way to win that war is to win it in Congress by passing a reform that has a shot at creating con-

fidence in the system. So the employer piece is a significant piece of that. The honest answer is that nobody really knows if we can make it work or not. We are a good ten to fifteen years away from the data being accurate enough. But there isn't an argument to be made anymore that we shouldn't be making the investment in getting the data to be accurate. And so for us, the question is now more about how to get there and what kind of protections do we need to fight to the death for.

In the current debate, the real fault line appears to be the temporary worker issue, with NCLR leading in the compromise position and with LULAC and other grassroots groups maintaining their opposition. On the left within the Hispanic community, there is considerable opposition to NCLR's approach. NCLR's staff member explains:

And so it is because we are in this place where we badly need solutions to the problem of undocumented workers and because of the death toll at the border, in some ways the bigger reversal in our position, in NCLR's position, and in the community position would not be our reluctant embrace of employer sanctions. It is the absolute reversal of our position on temporary workers. For fifteen years, whenever a guest worker position came up, our job was to kill it. And it came up a lot in agriculture; and we succeeded in killing it, every time. But a couple of things have happened. One is that the farmworker union has shown a willingness to compromise in order to make something positive happen for farmworkers who want to legalize. So the combination of that conversation happening, the growing discomfort with the death toll at the border, and the increasing ugliness of the immigration debate and the impact it has on the people, that combination brought us to the table on a temporary workers program. And we basically reached the conclusion that we needed a solution for people who would be coming in the future. That we are going to slam the door and that no one is going to come in is just unrealistic. The moral thing to do, given the death toll at the border, is get in front of the temporary worker debate, not have it shaped by employers, but to shape it ourselves. The way we thought of it was, "OK, let's break the mold here." So we have this nasty history with the temporary workers program. But we know there are going to be workers coming in, and rather than have them cross here in the desert and get into a climate that is going to be hostile, let's create a legal path for people.

While NCLR, as in the charter schools debate, based its decision-making on an analysis of the issue, a consideration of the possible policy alternatives, and an assessment of the political climate, organizations such as LULAC that are closer to the grassroots are somewhat limited in their ability to act in such a detached manner. NCLR leadership recognizes this:

> LULAC and MALDEF are kind of getting tackled by everybody. I think they are in a very reasonable place, because the legislative debate is pretty important, and we very much have to win. So MALDEF is in LA. Most of the center of gravity of the Left is in LA. And in order to preserve your relationships in LA, you have to—you can't be picking fights with people. I think MALDEF is going to try not to alienate anybody. But at the end of the day, their DC office and their leadership has legislative experience; they know what it takes to pass bills. . . . For LULAC, it's a little different. They have new leadership every two years. So every two years is different. But they have quite an outspoken new president and I think they want to be relevant to the debate. I think they want to be relevant to what's happening in Congress.

Evidence suggests that in early 2007, LULAC leadership did appear to be somewhat more focused on LULAC's relevance in Washington. The immigration plank of its legislative platform reflects a willingness to compromise that represents a departure from its earlier positions on immigration and other issues:

> LULAC opposes any legislation that threatens the rights of immigrants, criminalizes them or those who provide them assistance, and harms Latino communities. LULAC opposes harsh regulations that toughen the requirements for citizenship and stipulations that raise the bar of admissibility for immigrants. Immigrant visas should not be unreasonably withheld. Legal residents and naturalized citizens should have the same benefits due native-born citizens. LULAC opposes the militarization of the border and vigilante attacks on immigrants, as well as the mistreatment of immigrants in the United States regardless of their status. LULAC supports the regularization of undocumented workers in the United States by periodically updating the Date of Registry, the reinstatement of Section 245(i) to allow immigrants to remain with their families while their applications are processed, along with the restoration of food stamps for legal immigrants. LULAC supports citizenship for America's noncitizen troops. LULAC supports strong family reunification standards

and fair and balanced immigration processes to take into account future flows of workers. LULAC urges Congress to pass
wage protection for immigrants, as well as to mitigate the Hoff-
man decision. Though LULAC does not support guest-worker
programs, should they pass, LULAC endorses full worker protections, including the right to organize and to apply for citizenship on their own right without depending on their employer.
LULAC opposes the use of local law enforcement to assist the
DHS [Department of Homeland Security].

The bulk of its position is not surprising, given its strong support of immigrants in recent years and its unwillingness to compromise. Its statement on
guest-worker programs, however, does reflect a softening of its position.
This softening is not, however, confirmed in an interview with a top board
member, who maintains that LULAC's opposition to guest-worker programs is unchanged and considers its position to be very different from
NCLR's. This member says, "We don't want another Bracero program.
Immigrants need a process to citizenship. . . . We have always been against
a guest-workers program. We will be against them, but if they're passed,
then we have to deal with them." In February 2007 LULAC joined with
other grassroots organizations to ask that the new Democratic majority in
Congress make immigration reform a top priority, and announced plans to
launch a grassroots campaign to pressure members of Congress
(http://lulac.org/advocacy/press/2007/100daysletter.html). Campaign partners include LULAC, the Southwest Voter Registration Education Project,
the Hispanic Federation, and America Votes. The Hispanic Federation is a
coalition of about one hundred local groups, most based in the New York
area; the Southwest Voter Registration Education Project focuses on voter
education and registration in the Southwest; and America Votes is one of
the nation's largest liberal voter-mobilization groups. LULAC is not a
member of the Coalition for Comprehensive Immigration Reform, which
has been able to distribute funds to local groups for immigration advocacy
efforts. LULAC leadership reports that LULAC has received no funding for
their work on immigration. This is not the case with NCLR, a founding
member of the Coalition for Comprehensive Immigration Reform. In
2003, a major foundation approached several of the leading organizations
working on immigration reform and suggested to them that it would be
willing to invest in a comprehensive campaign to pass an immigration reform bill. NCLR, as one of the founding members, has played a role in dis-
tributing funds—several million dollars—to other groups at the local as
well as the national level who share the same core principles. The program
of the coalition is found on its Web site (www.cirnow.org) and can be summarized as follows:

- Comprehensive reform that would address admissions policy, which determines how many and which immigrants are allowed entry to the United States; incorporation policy, which deals with the extent to which immigrants are allowed access to federal programs and the citizenship process; and enforcement policy, which focuses on deterrence of illegal immigration
- Provisions for undocumented immigrants currently living in the United States to be eligible for permanent residence and citizenship.
- A dramatically revised temporary-worker program that protects workers
- An expedited process to reunite families caught in administrative delays
- Enforcement mechanisms that are effective and fair
- Resources to provide immigrants with English instruction and citizenship preparation

An NLCR staff member comments on why the funder got engaged and the impact funding has had:

> They essentially got persuaded that what it is we were trying to do could have a dramatic impact on the American landscape, and they wanted to invest in making it happen. But ultimately most of that money went out the door locally. There is no coincidence that the major, biggest rallies in the spring were really organized by groups that were very much part of this network. The other big, big sources of money were the unions. In order to get half a million people on the streets of Los Angeles, you need microphones and that kind of stuff. And the unions actually provided that kind of support. But the fact that everybody across the country carried the same sign, the We Are America sign, that was this campaign that literally produced this design and put it on the Web site. The fact that you had people in Memphis as [well as] people in Chicago and in LA. That's—money made that happen.

In response to the accusation that NCLR takes the positions it does based on funding, this staff member suggests that funders are impacted by the positions NCLR takes and explains why it pursues the strategy it does on immigration:

> Corporate funders are not really part of this conversation. They give NCLR general support, but there is not nickel of corporate money in our immigration work. We have money from a number

of foundations that support our immigration work. We are
making policy decisions based on what is good for the community, and what ends up happening is that our corporate funders
get attacked by the anti-immigration crowd. And the attacks
against NCLR have been unbelievable. Since 9/11, I think we've
lost ten to fifteen years of progress just on the notion of framing
Latinos as an American constituency. We now get reporters from
more reputable programs, from Anderson Cooper's program on
CNN, for example. Once, the first question in this interview was,
"Explain to me why the growth of the Latino community is bad
for the United States." Pop any other group into that sentence
and tell me it's not wildly offensive, and they wouldn't ask that
of the NAACP or of a Jewish group; there's just no way. And I
stopped him and I said, "Do you mean to ask if the growth of the
immigrant community is bad for the country?" And he said,
"Oh, no no no." And his follow-up question was, "Well aren't
your kids a burden in our schools?" And I could not get this guy
to see that this was an inappropriate question. That wasn't an
isolated incident at all. We just did a report on hunger in the
Latino community—this was about Hispanic children, the vast
majority of whom are U.S.-born and facing hunger. We released
it in December and the *Post* ran a piece on it. And the responses
were—"Well, just send them back to Mexico. They're here illegally anyway." We will never pass a bill on health care or education or anything else until we get the immigration issue off the
table. And our policies are being made for that reason. To advance the interests of the community, period. If anything, it's
making it much harder to do the core of everything else we do,
much harder. But we have to do this.

The criticisms come from both the Left and the Right. The above describes the right-wing position; from the left-wing, NCLR is criticized for
compromising on legislation. Here is this staff member's explanation:

Our policy judgments have been driven by what they always have
been driven by. We are trying to maximize outcomes for the community. And we are not going to win everything. Even if we are
wildly successful this year, the legalization program won't affect
every single one of the twelve million we want it to. We're going to
get clobbered on enforcement. There are going to be provisions.
And our job is to try to minimize those. We want to move forward
and get to the other side of the debate and face what we have to
face there. I really do think we've lost ground tremendously.

Conclusion

Two major issues have been the focus of attempts to reform immigration for decades: employer sanctions and temporary guest workers. On these issues, NCLR has distinguished itself by emphasizing its willingness to compromise. NCLR accepted the need to bargain in order to be part of the process, while LULAC maintained its positions on both issues. Two instances of their divergent opinions stand out: on employer sanctions in the 1986 immigration act and on temporary guest workers in the current debate.

From 1982 to 1985, NCLR and LULAC worked together in a coalition to oppose the 1986 immigration bill, which the organizations believed would result in increased discrimination against Hispanics. While they were initially successful in blocking efforts to pass a bill, by 1995 the momentum for bill passage was seemingly unstoppable. After assessing the political landscape, NCLR decided to compromise in order to maintain a bargaining position. LULAC, however, maintained its opposition. Similarly, in the recent run-up to a comprehensive immigration reform bill, NCLR has made clear its willingness to work on a temporary-worker program, while LULAC opposes any guest-worker program. Their positions complicate the picture of the assumed evolution of organizations from activist to more-conservative groups; LULAC is the oldest Hispanic national organization and has a conservative history, but, at least in the case of immigration, it maintains a fairly radical position.

As in the charter schools case, there is clear evidence of the importance of policy entrepreneurs. The position of a certain senior staff member played a key role in bringing NCLR to the table on employer sanctions, and the absence of a high-profile staff member very likely impacted LULAC's influence. Recalls an NCLR staff member: "LULAC has never had that kind of profile in DC since. One of those astonishing truths of the whole nonprofit sector is that personnel changes can change the profile of entire institutions, institutions with histories as deep and hallowed as organizations like LULAC or the NAACP. You go from being on the map to not on the map with the change of one person."

NCLR's decision-making on immigration reform over several decades is illuminated by considering activity in the problem, policy, and political streams. It is clear that NCLR, through research, analysis, and advocacy, is very cognizant of activity in each of the streams and watches carefully for windows of opportunity where it can be influential in moving the debate or particular pieces of legislation in a direction that is consistent with its goals. In contrast, LULAC's changes in position result from changes in leadership, and in those cases where NCLR changed position but LULAC did not, the influence of membership is likely to have played a role. As earlier chapters have indicated, once the legislative platform is voted on, LULAC leadership finds it very difficult to adjust its position on an issue.

7

Conclusion

N CLR and LULAC are considered similar organizations by many in Washington. Both claim to represent the Hispanic community, both have national offices in the nation's capital, both are involved in influencing policy-making, and both have local membership. Closer observation finds that the two organizations are dramatically different from each other. This final chapter summarizes the findings that result from application of the multiple-streams model and responds to other theories of interest group behavior, highlights the contributions of this study to the interest group literature, and offers conclusions.

Cross-Site Findings

Looking at the five elements offered by the Kingdon model illuminates the unique character of each organization. First, in the problem stream, the two organizations come to their definition of problems very differently. At NCLR, problem definition is influenced by a strong and well-respected policy analysis office, whose findings carry considerable weight with organizational decision-makers—members of the board of directors and the CEO. This contrasts with LULAC, whose leadership does not prioritize policy analysis, as evidenced by the lack of staffing to carry out such work. NCLR is also very interested in being at the negotiating table in Washington, and this drives its problem definition. At LULAC, members are not likely to tolerate a great deal of compromise. Thus, lack of participation in policy debates is not necessarily a problem. Despite these differences, the problem stream was a good predictor of activity in the policy stream for both groups. At LULAC, the identification of the high Hispanic dropout rate as a problem provided an opportunity for policy alternatives addressing that issue to rise in the policy stream. However, because of limited staffing and reliance on volunteers, policy alternatives are often one-dimensional;

149

a noncontroversial program or model that is spearheaded by an established member of the organization is likely to receive attention. If the model is a good candidate for funding, it is almost guaranteed attention. NCLR is less focused on fitting programs to sources of funding and more interested in the impact it has at the national level. This makes its decision-making increasingly multifaceted. In NCLR's policy stream, leadership responded to board members' desire to be active in current policy debates, the activity of prominent members/affiliates on particular policy alternatives, and an analysis of available policy alternatives on the national level.

The political streams of the two organizations are dramatically different, but in both cases were critical to the window of opportunity. In NCLR's case it allowed a window to open, while in LULAC's case it constrained the window's full opening. At NCLR, the decision-making is influenced by the policy alternatives being considered at the national level outside of the organization. Since it is ideologically flexible, it is willing to explore alternatives that other organizations might dismiss outright. As importantly, NCLR wants to be part of the national debate on policy issues, and it feels that the only way to be asked to the table is if it is willing to compromise. This is particularly evident in the case of immigration. By compromising, NCLR believes it will gain more than if it maintains more radical positions. At LULAC, activity in the political stream is centered on the political system within the organization, rather than on federal political leadership. Policy positions are strongly influenced by grassroots leadership, who are less willing to compromise their positions that are more ideologically based. As a result, LULAC's goal-formation process results in positions that clearly reflect the voice of the grassroots.

With regard to policy entrepreneurs, in both cases individuals who enthusiastically promoted their policy alternative were essential to the ultimate outcome, confirming Mintrom's (2000) work on policy entrepreneurs. At LULAC, Manny Isquierdo single-handedly developed a policy alternative that would address the dropout issue. At NCLR, senior-level and junior-level staff were critical players who strongly influenced the outcome of the charter school debate within the organization; individual staff members were also key during the employer sanctions debate.

Finally, the task force appears to be a common window of opportunity, though windows can open with the election of new leadership or political changes external to the organization. In NCLR's case, the task force was assigned the job of developing NCLR's position on the critical education policy issues of the day. In LULAC's case, as a result of staffing and internal political constraints, the task force really only reiterated the organization's positions on well-established education policy alternatives. In the case of immigration, however, a new president at LULAC appears to be pushing LULAC into a more visible national role.

With regard to the three groups of actors that potentially play a role in the goal-formation process of interest groups, funders were not found to be important, while members and leaders were critical to both organizations.

At NCLR and LULAC, local members heavily influenced the decision-making process, suggesting that organizations such as NCLR and LULAC enable local organizations to impact policy-making at the national level. At NCLR, affiliates that were older (ten years or more) and that were influential in their own right had more access to leadership and were more visible within the organization. They served as models for other charter school starters to follow and pushed NCLR toward support of charter schools.

Leaders at NCLR, whether they were paid staff or volunteer board members, strongly influenced the direction and the scope of the internal debate and outcomes. At LULAC, where leaders are also members, there was clearly an elite cadre of longtime members who influenced the direction of the organization. However, in the case of charter schools, the negative response to the issue appears to have come from the general membership, and leadership has been unable to change their opinions.

While the above suggests that leaders were important, it should also be noted that their roles were different from earlier theorists' predictions. Michels (1958) argued that organizational leadership would make decisions that would ensure survival of the organization, with little regard for member preferences. Ortiz (1991) makes a connection between Hispanic organization leaders' desire for organizational survival and career advancement and their approach to fund-raising. Neither of my case studies found evidence of this type of behavior among leadership. While NCLR leadership was interested in strengthening its presence in the national education and immigration debates, it did so with the goal of benefiting Hispanics in general and its membership specifically, rather than for the survival of the organization. Certainly in LULAC's case, member preferences were impossible to ignore.

Other research cited in chapter 1 would suggest that the availability of funding was what drove decision-making, particularly that of NCLR. Marquez (2003b) and Ortiz (1991) claim that an organization's patrons (organizations or individuals who provide operating monies, such as foundations and corporations) will have significant influence, or at least the organization's leaders will not go against their interests or preferences. But according to key staff, funding was not the main reason NCLR endorsed charter schools. In fact, pursuing funding for charter schools was a cause for concern, since the funders were conservative groups with whom NCLR had previously not fostered a relationship. Similarly a senior staff member suggests the positions NCLR takes on immigration make fund-raising in the corporate sector difficult. In LULAC's case, if funding were a factor, there would have been at least some consideration of the charter school issue. LULAC is not well funded, and charter schools presented an opportunity to obtain significant new funding. On immigration, funding has had no influence on its position.

The present book has explained goal formation in nationally prominent Hispanic interest groups, a neglected area of research. The empirical puzzle results from the varied responses to charter schools and immigration at two of the leading Hispanic civil rights organizations, National Council of La Raza and the League of United Latin American Citizens. My findings contradict those of earlier theorists who suggest that goal formation is purely a result of one variable, such as the desires of funders. In fact, the goal-formation process is complex and changing; multiple actors exert influence, and the strategies and processes evolve as the organizations mature over decades. My analysis has found that placing three categories of actors (funders, leaders, and members) within the agenda-setting framework developed by Kingdon illuminates the goal-formation process within interest groups and allows for a fuller understanding of the organizations and their actions.

This study concludes that no one group drives the goal-formation process; instead, differences in organizational structure impact the influence of a particular group of actors. While in neither case did members control decision-making, it is certainly true that LULAC's general membership strongly influenced leadership's ability to pursue policy alternatives. At NCLR, only key members seemed to exert considerable influence. Leaders, who in the case of LULAC are also members, do not appear to make decisions based on a concern for organizational survival or personal career advancement. In the case of NCLR, the organizational culture allows for longevity in staffing. As a result, staff are less concerned with personal survival and more interested in larger policy questions. At LULAC, leaders may want to make decisions that will ensure voter satisfaction at the general assembly, but they are constrained in their ability to make policy changes that are not already acceptable to the membership. Finally, funders appear to have little or no influence in goal formation.

The application of Kingdon's model to the goal-formation process within interest groups is, I believe, a significant contribution to the study of interest groups. Rather than focusing on one or another factor such as members or leaders, the model illuminates the complexity of the process and identifies the differences between organizations. While the model is no more predictive in the study of interest groups than it is in the public policy arena, it nevertheless allows for more accurate description of the behavior of groups.

Contributions

NCLR and LULAC, in their own right, are impressive organizations led and staffed by individuals who are dedicated to improving the lives of Hispanics in the United States. As this book has made clear, I believe in the value of gaining a nuanced understanding of these two leading national Hispanic organizations. In addition, this study confirms the neopluralist approach to the study of interest groups. As evidenced by this examination of two similar groups acting on the same issues, the contexts within which decisions are made are crucial. By employing the Kingdon model, the contextual factors are clarified. Social entities, like Hispanics in general, cannot be defined monolithically. Whereas other research has lumped NCLR and LULAC together as national Hispanic civil rights organizations, with presumably the same priorities and strategies, this study finds significant differences. NCLR operates fully "inside the Beltway," immersed in the Washington policy-making process. LULAC is more closely connected to the grassroots, whose opinions are reflected, unfiltered, by LULAC's national office. In addition, while NCLR's goal formation is influenced by each of the three streams in Kingdon's model equally, LULAC, an organization controlled by a network of members who are elected to leadership positions, is very much driven by its internal political process. While LULAC establishes its policy positions based on the views of its membership, at NCLR leadership is more willing to interpret the needs of the Hispanic community as a whole. This study is the first to apply Kindgon's model to goal formation within interest groups. Future research should apply the model to other groups, comparing their behavior on a single issue.

Kingdon's model clearly has applications to the study of interest groups. This has been thoroughly addressed in this chapter and in the individual case studies. Hopefully, this book has moved the study of interest groups forward, building on Rothenberg's (1992) Common Cause study and largely confirming the neopluralist approach offered by Lowery and Gray (2004). While the neopluralist approach advanced by Lowery and Gray certainly supports this view, their view of the stages required for organized interests to influence policy outcomes curiously misses the goal-formation stage. My analysis identifies this stage as one of critical importance. Studying the goal-formation stage contributes enormously to an understanding of the reasons an organization takes the actions that it does in other stages.

Rothenberg concludes, as I have, that only a thorough investigation of an interest group, which takes multiple contextual factors into account, can provide sufficient information to explain interest group behavior. This is also consistent with the neopluralist approach. It explains why other studies have been able to attribute behavior to member preferences, funders' desires, or leaders' priorities. A limited study of only one aspect of an organization will not produce a sufficiently robust analysis. As found in this study of LULAC and NCLR, attributing behavior to one actor misses a great deal.

Just as looking only at one part of an organization is insufficient, this empirical investigation of two interest groups reveals the limitations of a single case study. While there is clear evidence of the importance of understanding multiple actors and contextual factors, it is also the case that these two groups behave very differently. As a result of their histories, organizational structures, and missions, actors have considerably different degrees of influence within each organization. General membership at NCLR is not nearly as influential in goal formation as is the membership at LULAC. Similarly, NCLR's leaders, and particularly their paid leaders, exert much more influence than similar actors at LULAC. The comparison provides a more nuanced understanding of the behavior of groups than is possible in a single case study.

In addition to advancing interest group research, this study also has practical applications. Interest groups would benefit from applying the interest-group goal-formation model developed in this study to their decision-making. This study clearly has identified the benefits and liabilities inherent in the different decision-making models employed by NCLR and LULAC. In the case of NCLR, it is possible that the policy entrepreneur has too much influence, which may lead to decisions that are not in the best interests of the entire membership. It is certainly the case, for instance, that only the most established and sophisticated affiliates were able to take advantage of the opportunity presented by NCLR's entry into the charter school arena. Limited resources within the programs arm of the organization resulted in a programs office that was heavily focused on charter schools, leaving very little to offer affiliates who were not in a position to start a charter school. At LULAC, decisions are based heavily on member preferences. While this democratic process certainly has its advantages, the organization might have been better served if it had been able to factor in the external political environment and an analysis of all policy alternatives. These examples show the benefit to any interest group of using the interest-group goal-formation model to assess the strengths and weaknesses of its decision-making process.

Conclusion

How do these groups choose from among policy alternatives? At NCLR, the calculus includes NCLR's desire to influence national-level policy-making, extensive use of research and analysis to inform it decision-making, and an analysis of the external political environment, including not only the views of its members but also the needs and desires of the Hispanic population as a whole. LULAC has remained true to its roots, and the dominant force in its goal formation continues to be the will of its members at the local level. This is expressed through the annual elections and results in organizational leadership that tends to look inward for guidance rather than to the external political environment. LULAC plays a valuable role at the local level, providing a structure for individuals to organize and make contributions to their communities. It also serves as a leadership training program, providing individuals with important political and leadership experience. At the national level, LULAC's ability to influence policy-making is constrained by several factors. First and foremost, the critical role members play in setting their legislative agenda results in policy positions that are, as one respondent put it, "from the heart." Decisions are not informed by research and analysis and are not influenced by the dynamics of policy-making in Washington; and this leads to positions that are unvarnished and that directly express the feelings of individuals at the grassroots level.

Thinking back to the questions posed in chapter 1, what does this new understanding of these organizations tell us about whom they represent, and how accurately they represent the Hispanic population as a whole? Both organizations express in their mission statements a desire to improve opportunities and conditions for Hispanics nationwide, not just their membership. Both organizations have membership bases and both have a presence in Washington. What this study shows is the difficulty organizations like these have as they try to both be national advocates and reflect the will of their membership. Each group has found it really can only play one of those roles well; the other role invariably suffers. For LULAC, the democratic structure clearly limits the role it can play in Washington, unless the wishes of its particular membership on an issue happens to give leadership some ability to be involved in policy-making. However, as some of its staff and board have recognized, erratic positions make it less credible, and therefore less likely to have a place at the table reserved for it. For NCLR, the policy staff are comfortable with compromising when they feel it is necessary to move an issue forward, either to get closure (as in the case of immigration), or to be part of the discussion (as in the case of charter schools). They are frustrated that people at the grassroots level do not appreciate the difficult bargaining position NCLR often finds itself in, and so NCLR often feels as though its motives are misunderstood. While both organizations are likely to continue to try to be all things to all people, what this study finds is that they are not likely to be successful on both fronts.

Comparing the policy priorities of these two organizations to Hispanic public opinion, there does seem to be broad agreement between organizational priorities and Hispanic public opinion polls that education and immigration are important issues for Hispanics. There is less of a match when one looks at particular issues. For example, while vouchers were largely supported by Hispanics (at least by those who were familiar with the concept), LULAC's membership, which includes teachers and others with an interest in the public school system, were strongly opposed. Similarly, the positions NCLR has taken on immigration would not be supported by Hispanic public opinion.

NCLR and LULAC have evolved in the decades since their establishment by dedicated individuals. LULAC, born in the 1920s as a middle-class organization and focused on acceptance into the American mainstream, was influenced by the Chicano and civil rights movement in the 1970s and continues to behave in many ways like a classic civil rights organization. NCLR was originally intended to provide technical support to local groups but quickly set its sights on Washington. Now, under new leadership, it appears to be rededicating itself to local groups while maintaining its place in national negotiations. The evolution of these groups will be interesting to observe. If successful, NCLR and LULAC will, each in their own way, help the nation understand and respond to the needs of a large and growing part of our population.

References

Allen, J. 2005. *Charter school growth*. Washington DC: Center for Education Reform.

Alvarez, R. R. 1988. National politics and local responses: The nation's first successful school desegregation court case. In *School and society: Learning content through culture*, ed. H. T. Trueba and C. Delgado-Gaitan. New York: Praeger.

Angostini, M. 2003. *Veteran charter schools outperform non-charters on API*. Sacramento, CA: Charter Schools Development Center.

Associated Press. 2002. Census: Hispanic dropout numbers soar. CNN.com.

Baker, B. D., C. Keller-Wolff, and L. Wolf-Wendel. 2000. Two steps forward, one step back: Race/ethnicity and student achievement in education policy research. *Education Policy* 14 (4): 511–29.

Bangs, E. T. 1999. Who should decide what is best for California's LEP students? Proposition 227, structural equal protection, and local decision-making power. *La Raza Law Journal* 11 (113): 113–66.

Barrington, B. S., and B. Hendricks. 1989. Differentiating characteristics of high school graduates, dropouts, and non-graduates. *Journal of Educational Research* 82 (6): 309–19.

Bartolome, L. I. 2003. Democratizing Latino education: A perspective on elementary education. In *Latino students in American Schools: Historical and contemporary views*, ed. V. I. Kloosterman. Westport, CT: Praeger.

Baumgartner, F. R., and B. D. Jones. 1993. *Agendas and instability in American politics*. Chicago: University of Chicago Press.

Baumgartner, F. R., and B. L. Leech. 1998. *Basic interests: The importance of groups in politics and political science*. Princeton, NJ: Princeton University Press.

Becerra, X. 1995. Beyond ideology: Educating language-minority children through the ESEA. In *National issues in education*, ed. J. F. Jennings. Bloomington, IN: Phi Delta Kappa International.

Benveniste, L., M. Carnoy, and R. Rothstein. 2003. *All else equal: Are public and private schools different?* New York: Routledge/Falmer.

Bernal, D. D. 2000. Historical struggles for educational equity: Setting the context for Chicana/o schooling today. In *Charting new terrains of Chicana(o)/Latina(o) education*, ed. C. Tejeda, C. Martinez, and Z. Leonardo. Cresskill, NJ: Hampton Press.

Berry, J. M. 1994. An agenda for research on interest groups. In *Representing interests and interest group representation*, ed. W. J. Crotty, M. A. Schwartz and J. C. Green. Lanham, MD: University Press of America.

Bourdieu, P., and J. C. Passeron. 1977. *Reproduction in education, society, and culture*. London: Sage Publications.

Bowman, K. L. 2001. The new face of school segregation. *Duke Law Journal* 50 (1751): 1751–808.

Bridgespan Group. 2005. *Growth of youth-serving organizations: A white paper commissioned by the Edna McConnell Clark Foundation*. Boston, MA: Bridgespan Group.

Browne, W. P. 1977. Organizational maintenance: The internal operation of interest groups. *Public Administration Review* 37 (1): 48–57.

Campoamor, D., W. A. Diaz, and H. A. J. Ramos, eds. 1999. *Nuevos senderos: Reflections on Hispanics and philanthropy*. Houston, TX: Arte Publico Press.

Carr, M. C., and S. H. Fuhrman. 1999. The politics of school finance in the 1990s. In *Equity and adequacy in education finance: Issues and perspectives*, ed. H. F. Ladd, R. Chalk, and J. S. Hansen. Washington DC: National Academy Press.

CHCI. 2000. *National directory of Hispanic organizations*. Washington DC: Congressional Hispanic Caucus Institute.

Chubb, J. E., and T. M. Moe. 1990. *Politics markets & America's schools*. Washington DC: Brookings Institution.

Cigler, A. J. 1991. Interest groups: A subfield in search of an identity. In *Political science: Looking to the future*, ed. W. J. Crotty. Evanston, IL: Northwestern University Press.

Cockcroft, J. D. 1994. *The Hispanic struggle for social justice*. New York: Franklin Watts.

Cohen, M. D., J. G. March, and Johan Olsen. 1972. A garbage can model of organizational choice. *Administrative Science Quarterly* 17 (1): 1–25.

Cohen, M. D., J. G. March, and Carnegie Commission on Higher Education. 1986. *Leadership and ambiguity: The American college president*. Boston, MA: Harvard Business School Press.

Committee for Education Funding. 2003. *FY04 budget alert*. Washington DC: Committee for Education Funding.

Cooper, M. 2002. Charter schools: Will they improve or hurt public education? *CQ Researcher* 12 (44): 1033–056.

Cortes, M. 1999. A statistical profile of Latino nonprofit organizations in the United States. In *Nuevos senderos: Reflections on Hispanics in philanthropy*, ed. D. Campoamor, W. A. Diaz, and H. A. J. Ramos. Houston, TX: Arte Publico Press.

Crampton, T. 2004. After 30 years, Hispanic leader is retiring from advocacy group. *New York Times*, October 6.

Crawford, J. 2000. *At war with diversity: U.S. language policy in an age of anxiety*. Clevedon: Multilingual Matters.

Cyert, R. M., and J. G. March. 1992. *A behavioral theory of the firm*. Oxford: Blackwell.

de la Garza, R. O. 1988. Chicano elites and national policy-making, 1977–1980: Passive or active representatives. In *Latinos and the political system*, ed. F. C. Garcia. Notre Dame, IN: University of Notre Dame Press.

de la Garza, R. O., and F. Lu. 1999. Explorations in Latino voluntarism. In *Nuevos senderos: Reflections on Hispanics and philanthropy*, ed. D. Campoamor, W. A. Diaz, and H. A. J. Ramos. Houston, TX: Arte Publico Press.

Dillon, S., and D. J. Schemo. 2004. Charter schools fall short in public schools matchup. *New York Times*, November 23.

Dobbs, L. 2006. English only advocates see barriers to bill easing up. CNN.com. Washington DC, Electronic edition, April 19.

Donato, R. 1997. *The other struggle for equal schools: Mexican Americans during the civil rights era*. Albany: State University of New York Press.

Easton, D. 1965. *A framework for political analysis*. Englewood Cliffs, NJ: Prentice Hall.

Fischel, W. A. 1996. How Serrano caused proposition 13. *Journal of Law and Politics* 12 (4): 607–36.

Ford Foundation. 1975. *La Raza: Ford Foundation assistance to Mexican Americans.* New York: Ford Foundation.

Fordham, S., and J. U. Ogbu. 1986. Black students school success: Coping with the burden of acting white. *Urban Review* 18 (3): 176–206.

Fraga, L., K. J. Meier, and R. E. England. 1986. Hispanic Americans and educational policy: Limits to equal access. *Journal of Politics* 48 (4): 850–76.

Frankenberg, E., L. Chungmei, and G. Orfield. 2003. *A multiracial society with segregated schools: Are we losing the dream?* Boston, MA: Civil Rights Project, Harvard University.

Franklin, B. 1961. *The papers of Benjamin Franklin.* New Haven, CT: Yale University Press.

Fuller, B. 2000. *Inside charter schools: The paradox of radical decentralization.* Cambridge, MA: Harvard University Press.

Gallegos, H. E., and M. O'Neill. 1991. *Hispanics and the nonprofit sector.* New York: Foundation Center.

Garcia, F. C. 1988. *Latinos and the political system.* Notre Dame, IN: University of Notre Dame Press.

Garcia, J. A. 2003. *Latino politics in America: Community, culture, and interests.* Lanham, MD: Rowman & Littlefield.

Gill, B. P. 2001. *Rhetoric versus reality: What we know and what we need to know about charter schools and vouchers.* Santa Monica, CA: Rand Education.

Gomez, L. E. 1992. The birth of the Hispanic generation: Attitudes of Mexican-American political elites toward the Hispanic label. *Latin American Perspectives* 19 (75): 45–58.

Gonzalez, G. G. 1990. *Chicano education in the era of segregation.* Philadelphia: Balch Institute Press.

Gray, V., and D. Lowery. 1996. A niche theory of interest representation. *Journal of Politics* 58 (1): 91–111.

Green, D. P., and I. Shapiro. 1994. *Pathologies of rational choice theory: A critique of applications in political science.* New Haven, CT: Yale University Press.

Gross, A. J. 2003. Whiteness and others: Mexican Americans and American law; comment; Texas Mexicans and the politics of whiteness. *Law and History Review* 21 (1): 195–206.

Gutierrez, J. M. 1986. The political dynamics of bilingual education: A retrospective study of interest groups. Ph.D. diss., Stanford University, Sacramento, CA.

Hamann, E. T. 2003. *The educational welcome of Latinos in the new South*. Westport, CT: Praeger.

Hassel, B. 2005. Charter achievement among low-income students. Washington DC: Charter School Leadership Council.

Hassel, B., M. G. Terrell, A. Kain, and T. Zieberth. 2007. *Charter school achievement: What we know*. 4th ed. Washington DC: National Alliance for Public Charter Schools.

Henig, J. R. 1996. The local dynamics of choice: Ethnic preferences and institutional responses. In *Who chooses? Who loses? Culture, institutions, and the unequal effects of school choice*, ed. B. Fuller and R. F. Elmore. New York: Teachers College Press.

Hernandez, C. 1995. LULAC: The history of a grass roots organization and its influence on educational policies, 1929–1983. In *Department of Educational Leadership and Policy Studies*. Chicago: Loyola University.

Hero, R. E., and R. Preuhs. 2005. Minority advocacy group relations in a changing America: Policy concerns and positions in the congressional and legal arenas. In *American Political Science Association*. Washington DC.

Hero, R. E., and C. J. Tolbert. 1995. Latinos and substantive representation in the U.S. House of Representatives: direct, indirect, or nonexistent. *American Journal of Political Science* 39:640–52.

Herrnson, P. S., R. G. Shaiko, and C. Wilcox. 2005. *The interest group connection: Electioneering, lobbying, and policymaking in Washington*. Washington, D.C., CQ Press.

Hess, F. 2004. *School boards at the dawn of the 21st century: Conditions and challenges of district governance*. Alexandria, VA: National School Boards Association.

Howlett, M., and M. Ramesh. 2003. *Studying public policy: Policy cycles and policy subsystems*. Don Mills, ON: Oxford University Press.

Hunter, M. A. 2006. *State by state status of school finance litigations*. Washington DC: Campaign for Educational Equity.

Kaplowitz, C. A. 2003. A distinct minority: LULAC, Mexican American identity, and presidential policymaking, 1965–1972. *Journal of Policy History* 15 (2): 192–222.

Kingdon, J. W. 1984. *Agendas, alternatives, and public policies*. Boston, MA: Little, Brown.

Kloosterman, V. I., ed. 2003. *Latino students in American schools*. Westport, CT: Praeger.

Knoke, D. 1989. *Organizing for collective action: The political economies of associations*. New York: Aldine de Gruyter.

Lasswell, H. D. 1956. *The decision process: Seven categories of functional analysis*. College Park: University of Maryland Press.

Latin Insights. 2006. Inside the mind of Hispanic voters. Washington, DC. NDN.org.

LeMay, M. C. 1994. *Anatomy of a public policy: The reform of contemporary American immigration law*. Westport,CT: Praeger.

Lemus, G. D. 2002. LULAC national education agenda: Challenges and policy recommendations 2002–2003. Washington DC: LULAC.

Levin, H. M. 1990. The theory of choice applied to education. In *Choice and control in American education*, ed. W. Clune and J. Witte. New York: Falmer Press.

Lindblom, C. E. 1959. The science of "muddling through." *Public Administration Review* 19 (2): 79–88.

Lopez, I. F. H. 2001. Protest, repression, and race: Legal violence and the Chicano movement. *University of Pennsylvania Law Review* 150 (1): 205–44.

Malen, B. 2001. Generating interest in interest groups. *Educational Policy* 15 (1): 168–86.

March, J. G. 1999. *The pursuit of organizational intelligence*. Malden, MA: Blackwell Business.

March, J. G., and C. Heath. 1994. *A primer on decision making: How decisions happen*. New York: Free Press.

March, J. G., and H. A. Simon. 1993. *Organizations*. Oxford: Blackwell.

Marquez, B. 1989. The politics of race and assimilation: The League of United Latin American Citizens, 1929–1940. *Western Political Quarterly* 42 (2): 355–75.

―――. 1993. *LULAC.* Austin: University of Texas Press.

―――. 2003a. *Constructing identities in Mexican American political organizations: Choosing issues, taking sides.* Austin: University of Texas Press.

―――. 2003b. Mexican-American political organizations and philanthropy: Bankrolling a social movement. *Social Service Review,* September, 329–46.

Martinez, D. 2002. *State and local advocacy initiative case study.* Washington DC: National Council of La Raza.

Martinez, G. A. 1994. Legal indeterminacy, judicial discretion and the Mexican-American litigation experience: 1930–-1980. *U.C. Davis Law Review* 27 (3): 555–618.

McCarthy, J. D., and J. D. Zald. 1977. Resource mobilization and social movements: A partial theory. *American Journal of Sociology* 82:1212–41.

McKinnon, J. 2003. *The Black population in the United States: March 2002.* Washington DC: U.S. Census Bureau.

Meier, K. J., and J. Stewart. 1991. *The politics of Hispanic education: Un paso pa'lante y dos pa'tras.* Albany: State University of New York Press.

Michels, R. 1958. *Political parties.* Glencoe, IL: Free Press.

Milligan, S. 2004. New Congress is most diverse ever. *Boston Globe,* November 6.

Mintrom, M. 1997. Policy entrepreneurs and the diffusion of innovation. *American Journal of Political Science* 41(3): 738–70.

Mintrom, M. 2000. *Policy entrepreneurs and school choice.* Washington DC: Georgetown University Press.

Mintzberg, H., D. Raisinghani, and A. Theoret. 1976. The structure of 'unstructured' decision processes. *Administrative Science Quarterly* 21:246–75.

Moe, T. M. 1980. *The organization of interests: Incentives and the internal dynamics of political interest groups.* Chicago: University of Chicago Press.

Montejano, D., ed. 1999. *Chicano politics and society in the late twentieth century.* Austin: University of Texas Press.

Moran, R. F. 1987. Bilingual education as a status conflict. *California Law Review* 75 (1): 321–62.

Murray, C. 1997. *What it means to be a libertarian*. New York: Broadway Books.

NABE. 2003. NABE statement on president's 2004 budget proposal. http://www.nabe.org/press_detail.asp?ID=106.

National Council of La Raza. 1977. Minutes of the meeting of the board of directors.

———. 1999. *National Council of La Raza strategic five-year plan, 2000–2004*. Washington DC: NCLR.

———. 2005. *Raul Yzaguirre: A 30-year legacy remembered*. Washington DC: NCLR.

———. 2006. *Stronger communities, stronger America: NCLR 2006 annual report*. Washington DC: NCLR.

Navarrete, L. 2004. Latinos optimistic about future, feel candidates ignore their issues, and have a shared policy agenda, poll finds. http://nclr.org/content/news/detail/25333/.

NCLR. 1999. Positions on charter schools and vouchers. B. document. Washington DC.

New America Media. 2006. Great expectations http://media.newamerica media.org/images/polls/edu_poll/nam_edu_poll.pdf.

Nicolau, S. O., and H. Santiestevan. 1991. Looking back: A grantee-grantor view of the early years of the Council of La Raza. In *Hispanics and the non-profit sector*, ed. H. E. Gallegos and M. O'Neill. New York: Foundation Center.

Nutt, P. C. 1984. Planning process archetypes and their effectiveness. *Decision Sciences* 15:221–38.

Odden, A. R., and L. O. Picus. 2000. *School finance: A policy perspective*. Boston, MA: McGraw-Hill.

Olson, M. 1965. *The logic of collective action: Public goods and the theory of groups*. Cambridge, MA: Harvard University Press.

Orfield, G. 1986. Hispanic Education: Challenges, research, and policies. *American Journal of Education* 95 (1): 1–25.

Orfield, G., and J. T. Yun. 1999. *Resegregation in American schools*. Cambridge, MA: Civil Rights Project, Harvard University.

Orozco, C. E. 1996. Rodriguez v. San Antonio. In *The new handbook of Texas*, ed. R. Tyler. Austin: Texas State Historical Association.

Ortiz, I. D. 1991. Latino organizational leadership strategies in the era of Reaganomics. In *Latinos and political coalitions: Political empowerment for the 1990s*, ed. R. E. Villarreal and N. G. Hernandez. New York: Greenwood Press.

Orum, L. S. 1984. *Hispanic dropouts: Community responses.* Washington DC: National Council of La Raza.

Ospina, S., W. Diaz, and J. F. O'Sullivan. 2002. Negotiating accountability: Managerial lessons from identity-based nonprofit organizations. *Nonprofit and Voluntary Sector Quarterly* 31 (1): 5–31.

Ovando, C. J. 2003. Bilingual education in the United States: Historical development and current issues. *Bilingual Research Journal* 27 (1): 1–24.

Owens, A. 2006. *U.S. Hispanic Population: 2006.* Washington DC: U.S Census Bureau.

Padilla, F. 1986. *Latino ethnic consciousness: Case of Mexican Americans and Puerto Ricans.* Notre Dame, IN: University of Notre Dame Press.

Pew Hispanic Center. 2004a. *Pew Hispanic Center/Kaiser Family Foundation national survey of Latinos: Education.* Washington DC: Pew Hispanic Center.

———. 2004b. *Pew Hispanic Center/Kaiser Family Foundation national survey of Latinos: Politics and civic participation.* Washington DC: Pew Hispanic Center.

———. 2006. *From 200 million to 300 million: the numbers behind population growth.* Washington DC: Pew Hispanic Center.

Ramirez, R. R., and G. P. de la Cruz. 2003. *The Hispanic population in the United States: March 2002.* Washington DC: U.S. Census Bureau.

Rebell, M. 1998. Rodriquez revisited: An optimist's view. *Annual Survey of American Law* 1998 (289): 289–98.

Reed, D. S. 2001. *On equal terms: The constitutional politics of educational opportunity.* Princeton, NJ: Princeton University Press.

Reilly, J. F., C. C. Hull, and B. A. B. Allen. 2003. *IRC 501(c)(4) organizations.* Washington DC: Internal Revenue Service.

Robinson, T., and G. Robinson. 2003. Mendez v. Westminster: Asian-Latino coalition triumphant? *Asian Law Journal* 10 (161): 161–70.

Rodriguez, D. 2002. *Latino national political coalitions: Struggles and challenges*. New York: Routledge.

Rothenberg, L. S. 1992. *Linking citizens to government: Interest group politics at Common Cause*. Cambridge: Cambridge University Press.

Ryan, W. 2002. The Unz initiatives and the abolition of bilingual education. *Boston College Law Review* 43 (2): 487–520.

Sabatier, P. A. 1999. *Theories of the policy process*. Boulder, CO: Westview Press.

Sharp, E. B. 1994. Paradoxes of national antidrug policymaking. In *The politics of problem definition: Shaping the policy agenda*, ed. D. A. Rochefort and R. W. Cobb. Lawrence: University of Kansas Press.

Sierra, C. M. 1983. The political transformation of a minority organization: The Council of La Raza, 1965–1980. Ph.D. diss., Stanford University, Stanford, CA.

———. 1991. Latino organizational strategies on immigration reform: Success and limits in public policymaking. In *Latinos and political coalitions*, ed. R. E. Villarreal and N. G. Hernandez. New York: Greenwood Press.

Sosa, A. 1994. *Twenty years after Lau: In pursuit of equity, not just a language response program*. San Antonio, TX: Intercultural Development Research Association.

Suro, R., and G. Escobar. 2006. *The 2006 national survey of Latinos: The immigration debate*. Washington DC: Pew Hispanic Center. The Pew Hispanic Center bears no responsibility for the interpretations offered, or conclusions made based on analysis of *The 2006 National Survey of Latinos: The Immigration Debate* data.

Tatum, B. D. 1997. *"Why are all the black kids sitting together in the cafeteria?" and other conversations about race*. New York: Basic Books.

Therrien, M., and R. R. Ramirez. 2000. *The Hispanic population in the United States: March 2000*. Washington DC: U.S. Census Bureau.

Tierney, J. 1994. Interest group research: Questions and approaches. In *Representing interests and interest group representation*, ed. W. J. Crotty, M. A. Schwartz, and J. C. Green. Lanham, MD: University Press of America.

———. 1999. Polyglot city raises a cry for English. *New York Times*, August 16.

Tilly, C. 1978. *From mobilization to revolution*. Reading, MA: Addison-Wesley.

Trifiletti, L. L. 2004. The role of litigation in education reform: Holding California responsible, while preserving local control. *Loyola of Los Angeles Law Review* 38 (2): 549–67.

Truman, D. B. 1951. *The governmental process: Political interests and public opinion*. New York: Alfred P. Knopf.

Tweedie, J., D. D. Riley, J. E. Chubb, and T. M. Moe. 1990. Should market forces control educational decisionmaking? *American Political Science Review* 84 (2): 549–67.

U.S. Census Bureau. 2002. *Racial and ethnic classifications used in Census 2000 and beyond*. Washington DC: U.S. Census Bureau.

U.S. Department of Education. 2002. *The condition of education 2002*. Washington DC: U.S. Department of Education.

———. 2003. *Status and trends in the education of Hispanics*. Washington DC: National Center for Education Statistics.

Valdez, A. 1988. Selective determinants in maintaining social movement organizations: Three case studies from the Chicano Community. In *Latinos and the political system*, ed. F. C. Garcia. Notre Dame, IN: University of Notre Dame Press.

Valencia, R. R., ed. 2002. *Chicano school failure and success: Past, present, and future*. London: Routledge/Falmer.

Valenzuela, A. 1999. *Subtractive schooling: U.S.-Mexican youth and the politics of caring*. Albany: State University of New York.

Vanourek, G. 2005. *State of the charter movement 2005*. Denver, CO: Charter School Leadership Council.

Viadero, D. 2004a. AFT charter school study sparks heated national debate. *Education Week* 24 (1): 13–21.

———. 2004b. New data fuel current charter school debate. *Education Week* 24 (2): 17–23.

Villarreal, R. E. 1988. The politics of Mexican-American empowerment. In *Latino empowerment: Progress, problems, and prospects*, ed. R. E. Villarreal, N. G. Hernandez, and H. D. Neighbor. New York: Greenwood Press.

Villarreal, R. E., N. G. Hernandez, and H. D. Neighbor, eds. 1988. *Latino empowerment: Progress, problems, and prospects*. Contributions in Ethnic Studies. New York: Greenwood Press.

Walter, F. B., and S. R. Sweetland. 2003. School finance reform: An unresolved issue across the nation. *Education* 124(1): 143–50.

Wells, A. S., ed. 2002. *Where charter school policy fails: The problems of accountability and equity*. Sociology of Education. New York: Teachers College Press.

Wilson, S. H. 2003. Whiteness and others: Mexican Americans and American law; Brown over "other White"; Mexican Americans' legal arguments and litigation strategy in school desegregation lawsuits. *Law and History Review* 21 (1): 145–94.

Wortham, S., E. G. Murillo, and E. T. Hamann, eds. 2002. *Education in the new Latino diaspora*. Westport, CT: Ablex.

Yarab, D. S. 1990. Edgewood Independent School District v. Kirby: An education in school finance reform. *Case Western University Law Review* 40 (2): 889–904.

Zahariadis, N. 1996. Selling British Rail: An idea whose time has come? *Comparative Political Studies* 29:400–22.

Zahariadis, N. 2003. *Ambiguity and choice in public policy: Political decision making in modern democracies*. Washington, DC: Georgetown University Press.

Zolberg, A. R. 2006. *A nation by design: Immigration policy in the fashioning of America*. Cambridge, MA: Harvard University Press.

Index

AARP, 1
Affiliate Advisory Council, 69, 70
agenda setting process, 13, 14
Allen, J., 105
Alvarez, R. R., 92
Alvarez v. Lemon Grove, 92
alternative schools, 104, 112–114, 119
American GI Forum, 35, 98
Angostini, M., 103
Aspira, 27, 68, 111, 120

Baker, B. D., 4
Bangs, E. T., 100, 101
Barrington, B. S., 20
Bartolome, L. I., 103
Baumgartner, F. R., 3, 6, 7
Becerra, X., 67, 99
Benveniste, L., 102
Bernal, D. D., 91
Berry, J.M., 7
Bilingual education, 21, 34, 79, 86, 98–101
    Act, 75, 99
    California Proposition 227, 100, 101
    Charter Schools and, 104
    Public School program, 25
    Education Reform, 91, 98,
    Federal program, 27, 86, 90
    Interest groups activity on, 26, 78
    National Association of, 75
Bill and Melinda Gates Foundation, 101

Bourdieu, P., 20
Bowman, K. L., 91, 92, 94
Bridgespan Group, 86
Brown v. Board of Education, 26, 33, 93, 94
Browne, W. P., 7
Bush Administration, 49, 83

CAFTA. *See* Central American Free Trade Agreement
Campoamor, D., 31
Carr, M. C., 98
Castañeda v. Pickard, 99
CBA. *See* Corporate Board of Advisors
CBOs. *See* Community based organizations
census, 4, 75
Center on Budget and Policy Priorities, 80
Central American Free Trade Agreement, 58, 64, 66
Charter School Development Initiative, 86, 109, 119
Charter schools, 101–105
    Aspira and, 27
    Choice plan, 102, 103
    Goal Formation: NCLR on, 107–125; LULAC on, 125–136
    Hispanic Education Agenda and, 104, 105, 106
    History of, 25, 101
    in Hispanic educational reform efforts, 90–91

Charter schools (*continued*)
  introduction, 1, 17, 18
  LULAC on, 17, 49, 61, 66, 151,
    152, 153
  NCLR on, 2, 76, 78, 144, 151, 154
  Policy entrepreneurs, 148
  Raza Development Fund and, 70
  research on, 3
Chicano, 5, 31, 49
  movement, 48, 50, 90
  influence of, 156
Children's Defense Fund, 80
Chinese Exclusion Act, 137
Chubb, J. E., 102
Cigler, A. J., 4, 7
*Cisneros v. Corpus Christi Independent
  School District*, 94
Civil Rights Act of 1964, 98
Clinton, Senator Hilary Rodham, 1
Coalition for Comprehensive Immi-
    gration Reform, 145
Cockcroft, J. D., 33, 92
Cohen, M. D., 10, 11, 12
collective action dilemma, 6
Committee for Education Funding, 100
community based organizations, 2,
    19, 22, 24
  and advocacy, 26
  NCLR and, 67, 68, 80
  and charter schools, 90, 105
  and focus on education, 24
  and Hispanic education, 104, 115
Congreso de Latinos Unidos, Inc., 25
Congress
  Hispanics in, 22, 23, 26, 41, 64, 67,
    93
Congressional Hispanic Caucus, 23,
    67
contributors. *See* funders
Cooper, M., 101
Corporate Board of Advisors
  NCLR and, 69, 71, 87
  and education agenda, 85, 110
  and fundraising, 84
Cortes, M., 24, 25, 31
court cases, 26, 33, 67
Crampton, T., 68

Crawford, J., 98, 99, 101
Cyert, R. M., 11

de la Cruz, G. P., 19
de la Garza, R. O., 23, 31
*Delgado v. Bastrop Independent
  School District*, 33, 93
demand aggregation, 6, 29
desegregation
  LULAC on, 32–34
  MALDEF on, 26
  NCLR on, 67
  reform efforts, 91
  in court, 91–95
Dillon, S., 103
Donato, R., 48, 91, 92, 98

East LA blowout of 1968, 90
Easton, D., 11
education. *See under* Hispanic
    education
*Edgewood Independent School District
  v. Kirby*, 97
Elementary and Secondary Education
    Act, 99, 101
employer sanctions, 138–143
English Language Acquisition, 104
English-only, 79, 98, 100, 101
Escobar, G., 22

Fischel, W. A., 96
Food Research and Action Center, 80
Ford Foundation, 26, 34, 67–69, 94
Fordham, S., 21
Fraga, L., 23
Frankenberg, E., 95
Franklin, B., 98
Fuhrman, S. H., 98
Fuller, B., 102, 108
funders
  at LULAC: contribution statistics,
    59; fund-raising, 61; relationships
    with funders, 60
  at NCLR, 82–87: issues, 85–87;
    relationship with funders, 82;
    statistics, 83, 84; strategy, 85
  conclusions, 161

influence of, 30
Ortiz on, 31
in political stream, 15, 16, 17

Gallegos, H. E., 68, 74
garbage can theory, 10–13
Garcia, F. C., 90
Garcia, J. A., 6
Gill, B. P., 103
Gomez, L. E., 5
Gonzales, G. G., 80
Gray, V., 153
Green, D. P., 11
Gross, A. J., 49
group impact, 6, 7
guest-worker program, 140, 145, 148
Gutierrez, J. M., 31

Hamann, E. T., 5
Hart-Cellar Immigration Act, 137
Hassel, B., 103
Hayakawa, Senator S. I., 100
Heath, C., 9
Hendricks, B., 20
Henig, J. R., 102
Hernandez, C., 33, 34, 36, 48
Hernandez, N. G., 103
Hero, R. E., 23, 27
Herrnson, P. S., 4
Hess, F., 23
Hispanic
   education: attainment, 20; charter
      school agenda, 107; differences
      between subgroups, 5; history,
      18; poll results on, 21; reform
      efforts, 90, 103–105; school
      board on, 23
   definition of, 4–6
   population estimates, 19–22
   shared characteristics of, 5
Hispanic Federation, 26, 145
Howlett, M., 4
Hunter, M. A., 90, 98

illegal immigration, 21, 52, 138, 142,
   146. See also immigration,
   undocumented

immigration
   census data on, 5
   current immigration debate,
      141–148
   LULAC goal formation on,
      139–145, 148
   NCLR goal formation on, 139–143,
      146, 147, 148
   reform, 26, 27, 75, 88, 137–140
   undocumented, 19–22, 47–49, 138,
      139
Immigration Reform and Control Act
   of 1986, 75, 138, 139, 141
incentive theory, 30
Independent School District v.
   Salvatierra, 33, 91
interest group theory, 82, 110
interest groups
   definition of, 3, 4
   Hispanic, 26, 27
   historical review of, 6
   importance of, 1
IRS, 39, 45, 46
Isquierdo, Manny, 132, 150

Johnson, Lyndon, 99
Jones, B. D., 3

Kamasaki, C., 72
Kaplowitz, C. A., 33, 47, 47, 90, 98
Keyes v. Denver, 94
Kingdon, J. W.
   "black box" theory, 13
   five elements, 119, 149
   goal formation theory, 10, 88, 152
   multiple streams model, 3, 9, 12
   policy entrepreneurs, 14
   policy stream, 14, 153
   political stream, 15, 107, 119
   problem stream, 14
   window of opportunity, 16–17
Kloosterman, V. I., 103, 104
Knoke, D., 3

Lasswell, H. D., 12
Latin Insights, 21
Latinos. See Hispanics

Lau v. Nichols, 99
leaders
  at LULAC, 51–54
  at NCLR, 87
  Michels, R., 10
  model of goal formation and, 16,
    122, 135, 151
League of United Latin American
    Citizens. *See* LULAC
Leech, B. L., 3, 6, 7
LeMay, M. C., 140
Lemon Grove, 33
Lemus, G. D., 48, 133
Levin, H. M., 102
libertarian, 102
Lindblom, C. E., 11
Little School of 400, 34
LNESC, 59, 61
  activities, 34, 35
  funders, 59, 61
  national board influence, 38, 46
  role in education task force, 133
local groups. *See also* community
    based organizations
  activities, 24, 105, 109, 112
  in Hispanic Federation, 143
  representation, 22
  support from NCLR, 68, 156
Lopez, I. F. H., 89, 90
Lowery, D., 7, 8, 153
Lu, F., 31
LULAC
  annual national conference, 62
  as minority advocacy group, 27,
    89
  case study of, 32
  conference, 59
  constitution, 40, 44, 45
  convention, 56, 64
  corporate alliance, 39
  election system, 58
  funders, 59–61. *See also* funders
    main entry
  goal formation, 61–66, 127
  history, 32–38
  leaders, 51–54. *See also* Leadership
  Marquez on, 30, 36, 44

member influence, 49
members, 54–59. *See also* member
    main entry
misappropriation of funds, 36
national office: location, 37; match-
    ing funds program, 34; member's
    contributions, 54, 59; operations,
    42, 46–48, 63; staff, 32, 38, 39, 65
  on charter schools, 125–127
  on employer sanctions, 139
  on guest-worker program, 145
  on immigration, 144
  organizational ideology, 48–51
  organizational structure, 38–48
  paid staff, 47, 48, 52
  political structure, 40
  presidency, 42, 47, 49, 50
  problem stream, 127, 128
  tax status, 45
  volunteer strategy, 39, 40
  vouchers, 125–127
LULAC Foundation, 36, 46
LULAC Institute, 39, 46, 59– 61
LULAC National Education Services
    Center. *See* LNESC

MALDEF
  as minority advocacy group, 27, 68,
    94, 97, 120
  as radical organization, 48, 50
  initial funding, 34
  on employer sanctions, 139
  on immigration, 144
Malen, B., 8
March, J. G., 10–12
Marquez, B.
  on interest group behavior, 10, 29,
    31, 124
  on LULAC, 30, 36, 44, 46, 136
Martinez, D., 25
McCarthy, J. D., 4
McKinnon, J., 19
Meier, K. J., 23, 94
members
  at LULAC, 54–59
  at NCLR, 80–82
  conclusions, 151

in problem stream, 14
preferences, 9, 10
Mendez v. Westminster School District, 33
methodology, 17, 18
Mexican American Legal Defense and Educational Fund. *See* MALDEF
Michels, R., 10, 29, 151
Milligan, S., 23
Mintrom, M., 14
Mintzberg, M., 11
Moe, T. M., 7, 10, 102
Montejano, D., 90
Moran, R. F., 100, 101
multiple streams, 9, 12, 13, 149
Murguia, J., 81
Murillo, E. G., 5
Murray, C., 102

NAACP, 26, 67, 94, 147, 148
NABE, 75, 101
National Association of Bilingual Education. *See* NABE
National Council of La Raza. *See* NCLR
National Hispanic Task Force on Immigration Policy, 139
national identification card, 143
National Origins Act, 137
Navarrete, L., 21, 22
NCLR
    affiliate council, 80
    affiliates, 70, 76, 80
    annual budget, 83
    as minority advocacy group, 27
    board members, 87
    board of directors, 71
    CEO, 87
    corporate interests, 84
    education policy, 76
    funders, 82–87
    funding strategy, 31
    ideology, 77, 78–79
    leaders, 87
    members, 80–82
    on employer sanctions, 139

Office of Research, Advocacy, and Legislation, 72, 87
organizational history, 67–68
paid leadership, 87
policy analysts, 72
response to charter schools, 107, 109
Neighbor, H. D., 103
New America Media, 21
Nicolau, S. O., 78
No Child Left Behind, 65, 101
Nutt, P. C., 11

O'Neil, M., 68
Odden, A. R., 96
Olsen, J., 10, 11, 12
Olson, M., 6, 29
Operation Hold the Line, 141
Operation Wetback, 139
Orfield, G., 21, 93
organization theory, 9–11
Orozco, C. E., 96
Ortiz, I. D., 10, 31, 84, 151
Orum, L. S., 23, 104
Ospina, S., 31, 69
Ovando, C. J., 101
Owens, A., 5, 19

Parent Institute for Quality Education, 25
Passeron, J. C., 20
patrons. *See* funders
Pew Hispanic Center, 19, 21, 22
Picus, L. O., 96
Padilla, F., 5, 6, 85
Padres Unidos, 25
Plessy v. Ferguson, 93
policy entrepreneurs
    in agenda-setting, 13–15, 105
    in NCLR, 105, 117, 120, 122, 124
    in LULAC, 132, 140
    NCLR and LULAC comparison, 17, 148, 150, 154
policy stream
    in NCLR, 109, 111, 112, 115, 121
    in LULAC, 128, 129, 131, 134, 135
    NCLR and LULAC comparison, 149, 150

political activity, 4,13
political stream
    at NCLR, 109, 110, 119–122, 148
    at LULAC, 134–135
    for agenda-setting, 15–17
    for goal formation, 121, 134, 135
    NCLR and LULAC comparison,
        150
polling data, 19, 21, 22, 121
    English Only, 68, 100
Preuhs, R., 27
problem stream
    in agenda-setting, 14–17
    in NCLR, 110, 111, 115, 118,
        121
    in LULAC, 127, 134
    NCLR and LULAC comparison,
        149
Project SER, 35, 46, 59
Proposition 227, 100

Raisinghani, D., 11
Ramesh, M., 12
Ramirez, R., 19, 20
rational choice theory, 11
Raza Development Fund, 70,
    111–115
Reagan Administration, 69, 74, 82
Rebell, M., 97
Reed, D. S., 95, 97
Reilly, 45
Republican Party, 48, 49, 102
residential segregation, 90, 95
Riley, D. D., 102
Robinson, G., 92, 93
Robinson, T., 92
Robles, B., 36
Rodriguez v. San Antonio, 96, 97
Rodriguez, D., 31
Rothenberg, L. S., 7–11, 17, 153
Ryan, W., 98, 100

Sabatier, P. A., 10, 12, 13
Santiestevan, H., 78
Schemo, D. J., 103
school boards
    Hispanics on, 23

school finance reform, 95–98
segregation
    in court, 91–95
    LULAC on, 32–34
    reform efforts, 90
Select Commission on Immigration
    and Refugee Policy, 138, 139
SER Jobs for Progress, 38
Serna v. Portales, 99
Serrano v. Priest, 95, 96, 98
Shapiro, I., 11
Sierra, C. M.G., 49, 69, 140
Simon, H. A., 11
social movement organizations, 4, 30,
    31
Sosa, A., 99
Southwest Voter Registration Project,
    68
Stages (theory of policy process),
    11–12
Stewart, J., 23, 94
Suro, R., 22
Sweetland, S. R., 98

task force, 38
    as windows of opportunity, 150
    in LULAC, 127, 129, 132–135
    in NCLR, 71, 85, 115–117,
        120–123
    on education, 17
    on immigration policy, 139
    on international policy, 71
    on women, 71
Tatum, B. D., 6
teachers unions, 111, 117
temporary worker issue, 143
Terrell, Sharp, E. B., 15
Texas Court of Civil Appeals, 91
Theoret, A., 11
Therrien, M., 20
Tierney, J., 4, 7, 100
Tilly, C., 4
Tolbert, C. J., 23
Torrez, A., 139
Treaty of Guadalupe Hidalgo, 89,
    91
Trifiletti, L. L., 96

Truman, D. B., 6
Tweedie, J., 102

U.S. Census Bureau, 4, 5, 20
U.S. Department of Education, 20, 25,
    103, 104
Unz, Ron, 100

Valdez, A., 31
Valencia, R. R., 103
Valenzuela, A., 20
Valverde Elementary School, 25
Vanourek, G., 101
Viadero, D., 103
Villarreal, R. E., 89, 90, 103
vouchers
    board members on, 114–120
    conclusions, 156
    conjoined with charters, 102, 103,
        110
    LULAC on, 125, 126, 127
    political stream, 134, 135
    poll reports on, 21

Walter, F. B., 98
Wells, A. S., 111
welfare reform, 75

*West Orange-Cove Consolidated ISD
    v. Nelson*, 97
Wilson, S. H., 36, 93, 94
window of opportunity
    contrast between NCLR and
        LULAC, 150
    definition, 15
    for charter schools, 109, 125
    for education policy, 120, 123, 129,
        130, 135
    for education task force, 115, 122,
        127, 132, 135
    framework for study, 17
Wortham, S., 5

Yarab, D. S., 96, 97
Ylvisaker, P., 68
Yun, J. T., 93
Yzaguirre, Raul
    as member of LULAC, 41
    as president of NCLR, 69, 71–75,
        90–92, 112, 115
    on NCLR history, 84
    on Corporate Board of Advisors,
        81

Zald, J. D., 4